A.T.Q. STEWART was born in Belfast, where he was educated at the Royal Belfast Academical Institution and Queen's University. After some years in teaching, he returned to Queen's as a lecturer, and was appointed Reader in Irish History in 1975. He took early retirement in 1990 to devote more time to writing, and he is a frequent broadcaster on radio and television. He was consultant to both BBC Television's *The History of Ireland* and Thames Television's *The Troubles* and was a presenter for the Channel 4 series *The Divided Kingdom*. Since 1970 he has contributed to many encyclopedias and works of reference, prepared sets of questions for the BBC *Mastermind* series, and written articles for newspapers and journals, including the *Spectator*, the *Irish Arts Review*, *History Ireland*, the *Irish Times, Irish Independent, Sunday Tribune* and the *Belfast Telegraph*. His publications include *The Ulster Crisis: Resistance to Home Rule, 1912–14* (Faber and Faber, 1967; reissued by Blackstaff Press, 1997), *The Pagoda War: Lord Dufferin and the Fall of the Kingdom of Ava* (Faber and Faber, 1972), *The Narrow Ground: Aspects of Ulster 1609–1969* (Faber and Faber, 1977; reissued by Blackstaff Press, 1997), *Edward Carson* (Gill and Macmillan, 1982; reissued by Blackstaff Press, 1997), *A Deeper Silence: The Hidden Origins of the United Irishmen* (Faber and Faber, 1993) and *The Summer Soldiers: The 1798 Rebellion in Antrim and Down* (Blackstaff Press, 1995). In 1977 he was a joint winner of the first Christopher Ewart-Biggs Memorial Prize for *The Narrow Ground*. He is married with two sons and lives in Belfast.

EDWARD CARSON

•

A.T.Q. STEWART

THE
BLACKSTAFF
PRESS

BELFAST

First published in 1981 by
Gill and Macmillan Limited
This Blackstaff Press edition is a photolithographic facsimile
of the first edition printed by
Redwood Burn Limited, Trowbridge, Wiltshire

This edition published in 1997 by
The Blackstaff Press Limited
3 Galway Park, Dundonald, Belfast BT16 0AN, Northern Ireland

Printed by in Ireland by ColourBooks Limited

A CIP catalogue record for this book
is available from the British Library

ISBN 0-85640-613-9

Contents

Introduction   1

1. An Irish Barrister   3

2. 'Coercion Carson'   19

3. The Guiding Star   31

4. Sir Edward   57

5. 'King Carson'   77

6. Facing the Music   93

7. Betrayal   122

References   135

Select Bibliography   139

Index   143

Acknowledgments

I am grateful to the Keeper of the Records at the Public Record Office of Northern Ireland, Mr Brian Trainor, for permission to consult and quote from papers in his care; to his staff for their courtesy, and in particular to Dr Peter Smyth, who assisted me in tracing material in the Carson Papers. My thanks go also to Mr Colm Croker and Mr J. L. Lord, who made many helpful suggestions in regard both to content and presentation, and saved me from not a few errors. For any which remain I am entirely responsible. The book owes much to my wife for her patient help and counsel, and to Mrs Heather Johnson, who typed the manuscript.

Introduction

On 3 June 1935 the French liner *Normandie* completed a record crossing of the Atlantic, her time between Southampton and the Ambrose Light being 107 hours and 33 minutes. Speed was the keynote of the age. In March Sir Malcolm Campbell had set up a new land speed record at Daytona Beach, Florida, by driving his *Bluebird* at a speed of 276.8 miles per hour. A pilot of American Air Lines crossed America from Los Angeles to New York in 11 hours 21 minutes and one second. Miss Amelia Earhart flew nonstop from Mexico City to New York in 14 hours 18 minutes, and Mr H. L. Brook flew from Darwin, Australia, to the south of England in seven days. An express train covered the distance from London to Newcastle in 3 hours 57 minutes and knocked six minutes off the record on the way back. A dentist from Cleethorpes swam the English Channel from Cap Gris Nez in 14 hours 48 minutes. It was an exciting year.

The human heart remained much the same as it had been in Old Testament times. Once again the shadows of war were creeping across Europe. Mussolini's troops invaded Abyssinia, and Hitler introduced national conscription. In Europe's westernmost island deplorable rioting broke out in Belfast after the Orange parades on 12 July, and by 21 July nine people had been shot dead and scores injured. In the garden of a large house in Kent an old man sat in the sunshine and brooded on these events. The [2] newspapers made him bored and restless, for they spoke to him of the human beehive whose ceaseless hum came to him faintly from the distance. It had been his whole life, and he was too feeble any longer to be part of it.

Miss Greta Garbo appeared in *Anna Karenina*, and Mickey Mouse appeared in colour. Dr Sigmund Freud published his autobiography. Sidney and Beatrice Webb announced that Soviet Communism was 'a new civilisation'. It was the year of King George V's Jubilee. Miss Dorothy L. Sayers published *Gaudy Night*, which was a detective story; Mr T. S. Eliot published *Murder in the Cathedral*, which was not. The British government issued a white paper on defence. Mr de Valera supported sanctions against Italy. The League of Nations did not know what to do next. Summer ripened into autumn, and one October evening the newspaper placards in London said: 'LORD CARSON DEAD'. To the younger generation the news meant nothing; many of them did not know who he was. For older people the name revived memories they would have preferred to forget — the Great War, the Dardenelles campaign and the submarine menace, and, above all, Ireland: Ireland of the Ulster crisis, the Treaty and the 'troubles'. In Dublin, the city of his birth, he was not forgotten, nor in Belfast, where they had almost come to believe that he was immortal.[1]

1
An Irish Barrister

1

Edward Carson was born at No. 4 Harcourt Street, Dublin, on 9 February 1854, the second son of a modestly successful architect.[1] The Carsons were, as their name suggested, of Scottish origin. In 1815 William Carson moved from Dumfries to Dublin and established himself there as a general merchant. Of his three sons, two were educated at Trinity College and became clergymen of the Church of Ireland, remaining bachelors all their lives. The second son, Edward Henry, chose architecture as his career. In 1851 he married Isabella Lambert, the daughter of Captain Peter Lambert, who had an estate at Castle Ellen, some seven miles from Athenry, Co. Galway, and who could claim descent from Cromwell's major-general 'Honest John' Lambert, the blunt Yorkshire-man who helped to install Oliver as Lord Protector of the realm on the breaking up of the Westminister parliament in 1653.

There were elements in this ancestry which pointed to Carson's future politics, but the hints are perhaps misleading. Although he was to be, for the most dramatic part of his career, the 'uncrowned king of Ulster', his roots were entirely in southern Ireland. His mother was, beyond doubt, the most important influence on his life and career. When he was dying he told his friend the Archbishop of Armagh that he had seen much to shake his faith, and what remained was what he had learned at her knee: 'God so loved the

world that He gave His only begotten Son.'[2] Her
[4] photograph shows an amply proportioned Victorian
lady with an open, determined countenance and the
strong plain features which her son so markedly inherited. She was described as having blue eyes, dark
hair and a clear complexion — 'a regular Lambert' —
while Edward Carson senior was of medium build,
fair-haired and good-looking.

Isabella Carson bore her husband four sons and
two daughters. Before long No. 4 Harcourt Street
proved too small for the growing family, and the
Carsons moved into a larger house further along the
street. The children played in St Stephen's Green,
then still a private park. Almost from infancy 'Ned'
stood out in the family. He was taller than the others,
though not as robust, and already displayed something of that manic-depressive mixture of reserve and
high spirits which was so much a part of his later
character. He showed an early aptitude for drawing
and spent many happy hours in the architect's office,
which was at the back of the house, but already his
father had decided for some reason that this son
should pursue a career as a barrister.

His education began only a few doors from home,
under the benign guidance of a Church of Ireland
clergyman, the Rev. James Rice. A schoolfellow
remembered that he delighted in learning to recite
long extracts from the speeches of Burke, Sheridan
and the Younger Pitt, a presage of the oratory to
come. At the age of twelve he was sent, with two
of his brothers, to a boarding school at Portarlington.
The headmaster at Arlington House, the Rev. F. H.
Wall, who had just taken over from his father, became
not only his mentor but his lifelong friend. He may
have discerned some sign of future greatness in the
young Carson, but if so, it was not apparent to anyone else, for Ned Carson was not a brilliant scholar.

He worked hard, though, and in the sixth form began to show some inclination to the classics. Unlike his [5] brothers, he took little interest in sport and was excused games because of his weak constitution. A tall, ungainly lad, he quickly earned the nickname of 'Rawbones' and signed letters to his friends 'Bones' or, in schoolboy Latin, 'Ossa'. At Portarlington he learned to fend for himself and developed the combativeness, deep sense of loyalty and fierce detestation of injustice which were to be characterised in his legal and political career.

The family were anxious that Ned should follow the example of his bachelor uncles and go up to Trinity. He therefore sat the entrance examination in the summer of 1871, the same year in which J. P. Mahaffy was appointed to the Chair of Ancient History at the age of thirty-two. A mocking destiny decreed that in this entrance examination a boy from Portora Royal School, the son of the distinguished Dublin eye-specialist Sir William Wilde, should carry off all the academic prizes. Oscar Wilde then took a scholarship, and thenceforward his name appeared always in the first-class honours list until he departed in a blaze of academic glory to Oxford and further triumphs. Carson, who gained only a moderate place in classics, was by contrast a dull if conscientious plodder, apparently lacking most of Wilde's gifts. Contrary to popular legend, Carson and Wilde were never friends at Trinity; and although they were on speaking terms, Carson disliked and mistrusted the brilliant young aesthete.

While at Trinity Carson lived at home with his parents, walking every morning through St Stephen's Green and along Grafton Street to College Green. He enjoyed life as an undergraduate and became more interested in outdoor pursuits, going on the river with the University Boat Club, swimming at Sandycove

and even playing the recently revived game of hurling.
[6] And he could be boisterous. In 1876 he narrowly avoided rustication when, on the state entry of the Duke of Marlborough as Lord Lieutenant, he climbed the college railings and threw lighted squibs into the crowd. Typically, he refused to feign repentance and was saved only on the plea of his classics tutor.

In old age Carson declared: 'I have no more pleasant recollection in my life than my career in Trinity College, Dublin, and especially in the College Historical Society.' He joined the 'Hist' in his third year at the university, but it was not until he had taken his BA and was a postgraduate law student that his name began to figure in its records. The 'Hist', founded by Burke in the eighteenth century, was the oldest university debating society in the British Isles, and its membership had included Grattan, Wolfe Tone, Robert Emmet, W. E. H. Lecky and Isaac Butt. In 1873, when Carson first joined it, the auditor was a remarkable red-haired giant called Abraham Stoker. The son of a Dublin clerk, Stoker had won his way to the university and was renowned for his prowess as an athlete. Many years were to elapse before Bram Stoker terrified the world with *Dracula*, though the legend persists that this tale of horror was largely composed in his rooms at Trinity.[3] The minute books of the society bear testimony to the unexpected radicalism of the young Carson's opinions. He was in favour of women's rights and the abolition of capital punishment; he approved of the disestablishment of the Church of Ireland, denounced Cromwell and applauded the French Revolution. His speeches impressed contemporaries by their ardent sincerity.

If he was not himself academically a high-flyer, he benefited from the friendship of many who were. His closest friend was James Shannon, a brilliant boy who had been with him at Arlington House. Shannon was to die tragically young, but he had considerable influence on Carson. Of the others, James Ross would [7] one day be Lord Chancellor of Ireland, Charles O'Connor Master of the Rolls, and Richard Cherry Lord Chief Justice. Another lawyer, J. H. Campbell, would first be prominent in Carson's Ulster resistance to Home Rule and later, as Lord Glenavy, become the first President of the Irish Free State Senate. In 1876 Carson won the society's silver medal for composition and was elected librarian. A rare photograph of the officers of the 'Hist' taken soon after reveals an unfamiliar Carson, wearing a moustache and gazing away from the camera with the almost insolent assurance of three and twenty. But the ramrod back and determined features are unmistakably those of the later advocate preparing to cross-examine a difficult witness. On 20 December 1876 the minutes are signed impudently if prophetically: 'E. H. Carson, QC, Attorney-General'.[4]

2

It would be some time before the prediction was fulfilled, but already by 1877 Carson had found himself. He knew his strength and his limitations; and he was certain he knew where he wanted to go. In that year he was called to the Bar by the Lord Chancellor. Every candidate for the Irish Bar had to keep four terms in one of the English Inns of Court by 'eating dinners'. (Carson described this as 'one of the badges of servitude on the Irish nation'.) He chose the Middle Temple Hall, and before being admitted he had to obtain the signature of two English barristers 'lest he might steal the silver spoons'. In time he was to become treasurer of the historic Middle Temple, but for the moment his connection with it meant an uncomfortable sea journey four times a year. His

amitions did not extend beyond the Four Courts and
[8] the Leinster Circuit, where he served a thorough and
exacting apprenticeship.

In many ways life at the Irish Bar was a continuation of the club-like atmosphere of Trinity. The spirit
of the Ascendancy still hovered over the Bar library,
its traditions virtually unchanged from the days of
the great lawyer-politicians of the eighteenth century.
The Four Courts took its name from the fact that
opening off the main hall were the Chancery, Queen's
Bench, Common Pleas and Exchequer courts. Criminal trials for Dublin were held in the old courthouse
in Green Street, half a mile away. The Four Courts
building also contained the Bar library where the
barristers congregated. Curious and antiquated tradition, much of it just about to be swept away, domin-
ated the Bar practice. Barristers sat on forms at long
desks, or at the famous round table, or at the fire-
place, but since there were too many of them for the
available space, the atmosphere was that of an over-
crowded and noisy schoolroom. Uncomfortable as it
was, it bred tolerance and good humour, for without
these qualities the system could not function at all,
and this helps to explain why Carson remained in
later years on terms of such intimate cordiality with
many nationalist lawyers who deplored his politics.

A barrister was obliged to live in Dublin and come
to court regularly every morning. Robed and wigged,
whether he expected to be called into court or not,
he went to the library and worked on his papers. His
black brief-bag would have been carried from his
home by one of the 'bagwomen' such as the famous
'Snuffy Maggie', though these ladies were shortly to
be replaced by horse-drawn vans. In Dublin a junior
barrister had to be prepared to take a case or advise
proceedings in any of the courts; there was little
specialisation, and the wide experience gained was

immensely valuable to Carson, who later frequently astonished English judges by his grasp of abstruse legal doctrine. Without a clerk or private chambers, the Dublin barrister had to conduct his work in the bedlam of the library. What happened was that if solicitors or their clerks needed a barrister, they went to the door of the library, and the name would be shouted out in parade-ground tones by the 'crier', a burly ex-guardsman called Bramley. In time the young barrister learned to work in this din, impervious to all sounds except that of his own name. The library system had obvious advantages. Counsel could confer together informally, and juniors could ask for help from older, more experienced lawyers, while they had the opportunity to meet and study at close quarters the great law officers. In the library Carson made the acquaintance of Edward Gibson, the Irish Attorney-General, Lord Ashbourne, thrice Lord Chancellor of Ireland and a cabinet minister, and the great Isaac Butt, QC, the father of the Home Rule movement.

For a fee of fifty guineas Carson went as a 'pupil' to an experienced junior counsel, learning the art of preparing pleadings in civil suits, a skill which by all accounts he rapidly mastered. His first real case was provided through his father's influence. It concerned a building contract in which Carson senior had been engaged as architect, and the young Edward appeared for the defendant against whom the builder had brought suit. His father thus had the satisfaction of being examined in chief by his own son, tall and awkward in his new gown and wig. It also gave Carson his first experience of cross-examination, which was to prove his greatest strength. But most important of all, it brought him his first real earnings in fees and 'refreshers'. He later confessed: 'I lived for a long time on that case.'

His reputation as a barrister grew very slowly, but

his training was thorough and gave him the confid-
[10] ence to stand up to bullying judges, to hold firm
against seniors when he was in the right, to search
out the weaknesses in the evidence of lying witnesses
and to win over juries. His dogged persistence was
to have its reward in time. Right from the onset he
eschewed the temptations of brilliant rhetoric and
attempted wit. He said what he meant, and he early
showed an uncanny gift for asking the essential bed-
rock question, however obvious it sounded. He might
be given a rough time by judge or learned counsel, but
in the end they admitted he was right, because he
made sure he would be right. It left him with a rather
grim and combative countenance, occasionally trans-
figured by a smile when something appealed to his
quick Irish sense of humour. It was an exterior men
soon came to respect. 'The one thing about him that
impressed us all', wrote Ross, 'was his transparent
integrity and courage.'[5] Carson had a frightening
integrity.

3

During his undergraduate years Carson often spent
part of his vacations with his mother's relations at
Castle Ellen, and there he lost his heart to his cousin
Katie Lambert, a beautiful, high-spirited girl who was
a superb horsewoman and regularly hunted her father's
hounds. He even gave her his silver medal as a token
of his devotion, but the Lamberts had no intention of
allowing Katie to marry a penniless barrister. She was
unwilling to oppose her family's wishes, and Carson,
who was fiercely proud, did not seek to make her
change her mind. Some years later she married an
army officer and died in childbirth. By then Carson
had married someone else.

In the high summer of 1879, after a long day's
work in the courts, he and Shannon would some-

times go out to Kingstown or Sandycove and hire
a boat for an hour or two's sailing. One evening Carson
saw an attractive fair-haired girl, very smartly dressed,
watching the boats come in. Shannon had recognised
her, and Carson asked him who she was. Shannon
revealed that her name was Annette Kirwan and that
she lived at Kingstown with her father, a retired County
Inspector of the Royal Irish Constabulary. Shannon
was at first not anxious to introduce Carson to her,
but gave way to his friend's urgent pleading. Carson
fell in love with her at first sight. More meetings
followed, and very soon Carson asked Annette to
marry him. He was twenty-five and still living at home
with his parents, and he had no money apart from
£50 saved up in the bank. Not surprisingly, his father
was less than pleased when he was told of the engage-
ment. What would the couple live on? Annette was as
poor as Carson himself. Her mother had died when
she was young, and since her father's duties kept him
away from home at all hours, she was temporarily
adopted by a relative who was a Resident Magistrate
at Castlecomer, Co. Kilkenny, returning to live with
her father only on his retirement. On 19 December
1879 the young couple were married at Monkstown
parish church by Carson's old schoolmaster, the Rev.
Frank Wall, with Shannon as best man. The ceremony
took place very early in the morning, at eight o'clock,
so that they could catch the Holyhead mailboat, and
they spent their Christmas honeymoon in London.

When they returned, penniless, to Dublin they
were offered a home by Annette's relative, the Resident Magistrate, and in his house at Herbert Place
their married life began. At first it was an uphill
struggle. Few briefs came Carson's way, but when
they did he worked long into the night on them. When
he had no brief he sat up studying law, for Carson
could not bear to be idle, and nor could he bear the

thought of failure. Gradually the work began to come
in. If he landed a brief marked three or five guineas,
Annette and he celebrated with a visit to the theatre
or a day in the country. When a small house became
vacant at No. 9 Herbert Place Carson at once took it,
though he could scarcely afford it. There on 2 October
1880 Annette gave birth to their first son, William
Henry Lambert Carson.

Carson's marriage had been opposed by his family,
and especially by his father, who had even exchanged
'high words' with Annette's father. With that strong
will which was so much a part of him, Carson had
simply made up his mind and then acted. In time,
however, his father became reconciled and was, as is
so often the way, delighted by the arrival of his grand-
son. Edward Carson senior was taken ill suddenly in
1881, however, and died leaving his wife not well
provided for, and so the young barrister's responsibilities were considerably increased just as he was
making his way in the courts. His friend Shannon
outshone him in prospects and achievement. The son
of a solicitor, Shannon had work already created for
him. He had a first-class mind and splendid health,
whereas Carson was always ailing. It seemed likely
that he was destined for fame and fortune to which
Carson would never attain. Then out of the blue
Shannon was struck down by typhoid fever. Ignoring
all risk, Carson hurried to his bedside, and Shannon
actually died in his arms, exhorting him to 'Give up
the world, Ned, and meet me in Heaven.' Shannon's
young wife, who had pleaded with Carson not to go
in and see him, also died from the disease a few days
later. The death of his best friend marked Carson
deeply. He grew even more saturnine and more prone
to bewail his own indifferent state of health.

He seems indeed to have contracted the fever himself, but he was nursed through it by Annette, and in

his opinion she saved his life. Not long after he suffered another attack of illness, this time caused by [13]
gallstones. Carson boldly chose surgery instead of
medical treatment, though the operation was then
considered dangerous. It was successful, however, and
again Annette quickly nursed him back to health.
There were now two other mouths to feed, for a second
child, a daughter, Aileen, had been born on 13 November 1881. Fees are seldom paid on briefs until
weeks or months have passed, and Annette sometimes
found it difficult enough to meet the household bills.
Carson, who was toiling away all the hours that God
gave, was, and remained all his life, generous to a
fault, but he never really understood the value of
money and was too busy to be worried by such problems. His sister Bella had to remonstrate with Annette
for keeping all her financial troubles to herself. 'Surely
they are Ned's troubles as well,' she said.

The years of their early married life were disturbed
ones in Ireland. It was the time of the land war, when
murder and outrage became everyday events in some
parts of the country. In 1881 Gladstone's revolution-
ary second Land Act secured at last for tenants what
became known popularly as the 'three Fs' — fair rents
to be decided by judicial tribunal, fixity of tenure,
and free sale. The immediate result of this legislation
was a rush of work for the Irish Bar. Half a million
lawsuits followed, and whatever other benefits it conferred, Gladstone's act certainly brought substantial
rewards to lawyers. Carson had his share of these 'fair
rent' cases on the Leinster Circuit. At first he represented only tenants, but soon landlords recognised his
talents and their solicitors began to instruct him. It
brought much-needed money into his pocket and
enhanced his reputation — so much so that in Waterford the local nationalists approached him to stand
for parliament as a 'no rent' candidate enjoying the

support of the Land League. Carson declined the offer, [14] explaining that though he was a radical, he was also a firm believer in the Union between Great Britain and Ireland, which the nationalists were seeking to destroy. In any case, he still had a living to make.

4

Luck plays a substantial part in the career of every young barrister. If he is not to remain forever briefless, he needs at least one *cause célèbre* to make his name. Carson's came to him in a dramatic and amusing fashion. He was in bed one night in his hotel in Waterford when a wild-eyed middle-aged woman suddenly burst into his room and asked him to take her case. Having heard what she had to say, Carson referred her to a solicitor, and the latter in due course instructed him to appear for her. Miss Anthony was an eccentric lady who lived in Tallow, Co. Waterford. She had been detected travelling on the railway without a ticket, and an over-zealous porter had ejected her, none too gently, onto the station platform. She determined to bring an action against the railway company at the next assizes, and hearing that a 'counsellor' was staying at the local inn, she had lost no time in contacting him. Carson pleaded her case so well that the court awarded heavy damages against the company, but they then appealed, and Carson appeared for the respondent in a long-drawn-out lawsuit which again resulted in victory for Miss Anthony.

In the process she unfortunately developed a taste for litigation, dispensed with Carson's services and conducted her cases in person, with the result that she sometimes found, to her intense indignation, that he had been instructed to appear against her. On one occasion she vehemently attacked his personal character, adding for good measure: 'And your mother is no better than she should be.' The astonished Carson, more amused than angry, fell back, murmuring to his [15] solicitors: 'My poor saintly mother.' Miss Anthony went on to new triumphs. She first pledged a diamond ring with a Tallow tradesman to obtain a supply of bacon, and then issued a writ against him for illegally taking pledges, and so recovered her ring. Then she sued her parish priest for slandering her reputation by passing her over at the altar rails when she presented herself for Holy Communion. The priest, mindful of his own reputation, settled out of court for a substantial sum. Next she sued the local rate-collector for excessive collection. She lost this action, and, to save her goods from seizure, persuaded the Christian Brothers in Tallow to take her sheep into their field, borrowing money from them and subsequently suing them for return of her property in order to avoid repayment. The Christian Brothers, rather than go into court, sent back the sheep.

Flushed by success, she then made the mistake of turning on the legal profession itself. She served a writ for slander on a Dublin solicitor who had never heard of her. He imprudently threw the writ into his wastepaper basket, and as a result had £1,000 damages awarded against him 'in default of appearance'. At length he succeeded in getting the judgment set aside, but Miss Anthony was granted costs. Everyone was now so terrified of her that she became in fact a privileged person. The railway companies allowed her free travel, and tradesmen dared not sue her for unpaid bills, so she enjoyed unlimited credit. Eventually her mind began to fail, the Lord Chancellor's Lunacy Commissioner was approached, and she was committed to an asylum in Cork, where after a time she hanged herself. No newspaper even dared to report her suicide, for fear that she might have circulated the rumour in order to start a libel action. Carson had

taken no part in the proceedings which led to her
being certified, and he remembered with gratitude
that it was her first appearance in court which brought
him to public attention.

Carson's reputation was further enhanced when he
defended the two prisoners in a sensational Dublin
murder case. John Brennan and Thomas Martin were
charged with the murder of a young man called
Joseph MacMahon in a public house in Dorset Street.
The jury were unable to agree and were discharged.
The prisoners were brought up again at the next commission, and Carson offered a plea of manslaughter
which the Crown accepted. The case concluded only
a few weeks before the assassination on 6 May 1882
of the new Chief Secretary, Lord Frederick Cavendish, and the Under-Secretary, Thomas Burke, in
Phoenix Park, and it revealed a disquieting atmosphere in Dublin. That three young men of the artisan
class should be carrying revolvers in a pub in the centre
of the city, and that even a verdict of manslaughter
could not be obtained from the jury in the first trial,
shocked the judge, Mr Justice Lawson. Lawson had
no pity for lawbreakers, and later, after he himself had
been attacked by one of the Phoenix Park murderers
as he was walking in the street towards the Kildare
Street Club, it is said that he always sat in court with
a loaded revolver on the bench.

When Parnell and his lieutenants in the Land League
were imprisoned in Kilmainham jail under the Coercion Act in October 1881 they boasted that 'Captain
Moonlight' would take their place. It was no idle
threat. Murder and attempted murder became an
everyday occurrence. One of the worst outrages pre-
ceding the Phoenix Park murders had been the brutal
slaying of a Mrs Smythe at Barbavilla House in Co.
Westmeath on Palm Sunday, as she and her brother
were returning from taking Holy Communion in the

village church. Mr Barlow Smythe, the intended victim, was the Deputy Lieutenant of the county and a good landlord who had every reason to believe that his tenants were content and well disposed towards him. Over a year elapsed before the culprits were caught and brought to trial on the evidence of two informers. Dr Walter Boyd, senior counsel for the prisoners, left his junior, Carson, to make the closing speech.

Basing his appeal not on the evidence for the defence but on the unreliable nature of the prosecution's evidence, he suggested that the informers' account was a feeble imitation of what had appeared in the press in the Phoenix Park case. 'I would be as glad as any man to see the true culprits brought to justice,' he told the jury, 'but at what time in the history of this country has it ever been more requisite that jurors should be careful only to act on the clearest and strictest proof? No matter what abhorrence you feel for the crime, you must act on the evidence alone. You must not speculate, or attempt to find by speculation, a case against the prisoners at the Bar.' He implored them not to be led away by any desire of righting society: 'I hope it will right itself by fair means, but juries are not to be asked to convict innocent men in order that this desired state of affairs may come sooner.'[6] It may be noted that later, when Carson was himself the chief Crown prosecutor in Ireland, he never used the argument of 'the state of the country' to secure a conviction. He adhered strictly to the evidence of the crime in each specific case, without reference to the wider context of crime and politics.

Carson's address to the jury created a great impression throughout the country and was widely reported. It was an astonishing performance for a young barrister not yet thirty, and it made him famous. It also brought him to the attention of the Crown counsel, [18] Peter O'Brien, a fact of the utmost importance for Carson's subsequent career. O'Brien, a Catholic lawyer in his forties, had earned the nickname of 'Peter the Packer' because of the care he took with juries. It was virtually impossible in the early days of the Land League to empanel an unbiased jury, and O'Brien's fixed rule was to challenge every juror who appeared without a collar. He said, with some logic, that he really ought to have been called 'the Great Unpacker'.

Throughout these years of his early successes Carson's domestic responsibilities were increasing. At the end of 1885 Annette presented him with another daughter, Gladys Isobel, and Carson now decided to purchase a larger house in a more fashionable part of Dublin. In 1886 Edward and Annette Carson, with their three children and domestic staff, moved into a fine Georgian house in Merrion Square.

2
'Coercion Carson'

1

Gladstone's decision, at the end of 1885, that nothing
short of self-government would satisfy the demands
of the Irish people came as a shock to Carson, as it
did to many Liberals, who had assumed that the
Union at least was sacrosanct. But even the Tory
Lord Carnarvon, who was Lord Lieutenant while the
Conservatives were briefly in office from June 1885
until January 1886, had, in secret negotiations with
Parnell, held out the possibility of a *volte-face* on
Home Rule in return for the support of the Irish
Nationalist MPs. Early in 1886 Gladstone returned to
office as Prime Minister for the third time, but the
Liberal majority of 86 was exactly balanced by the
86 seats won by Irish Nationalists. Dependent on the
support of these MPs, Gladstone at once prepared a
Home Rule Bill for Ireland. On 8 April 1886, with a
large section of his party in revolt, he introduced it in
the Commons, and in June it was defeated by 343
votes to 313. Gladstone then went to the country,
and the electorate decisively rejected his policy. Lord
Salisbury again became Prime Minister and announced
his remedy for Ireland as 'twenty years of resolute
government'. With one short break, the Conservatives
were in fact to rule for twenty years.

The Home Rule crisis had shaken up the British
party system. The great Radical leader Joseph
Chamberlain led his Liberal Unionist followers into
the ranks of the Tories, while the Irish Parliamentary

Party became the prisoner of its pact with Gladstone
and the Liberals. Overnight most Irish Liberals, including a sizeable proportion of the Northern Protestants, declared themselves to be Liberal Unionists. For Carson, who had Liberal sympathies on many issues, the Union came first; it was, he later asserted, the guiding star of his political life. His political opponents in time to come were to allege that in 1886 he was 'an ardent Home Ruler', merely on the grounds that he had just been elected to membership of the National Liberal Club in London, and that he changed his politics when he saw which way the wind was blowing. But the charge seems to be groundless. There is ample evidence of his Unionism at this time — he was in fact campaigning for Liberal Unionist candidates in the July election — and the National Liberal Club was still trying to retain as many of the Liberal Unionists as possible.

Salisbury this time sent to Ireland as Lord Lieutenant the Marquess of Londonderry, who had been MP for Co. Down before succeeding to his father's title in 1884. The appointment of Londonderry, who was just thirty-four, was seen as a conciliatory gesture. Popular because of his sporting interests, he had in addition to rank and great wealth a beautiful young wife, Theresa Susey, the daughter of the Earl of Shrewsbury. A frequent attender at race meetings (a very unusual practice for ladies of rank at this time), she was also an intelligent and well-read woman with a taste for political conversation.[1] As Vicereine in Dublin she entertained with the assurance she was later to display when presiding over the last brilliant Tory salon in London. Among those who received invitations to the Castle and the Viceregal Lodge were Edward and Annette Carson. The meeting was momentous, for Lady Londonderry befriended Carson and took an interest in his career for the rest of her life. For the next thirty years she advised and encouraged him, was his confidante, and patiently listened to his constant complaints about his health and domestic circumstances.

An even more important connection, at least in the short term, was soon to be forged. Sir Michael Hicks Beach had been appointed as Chief Secretary, but almost at once he was forced to resign because of acute eye trouble. When Salisbury chose as his successor his own nephew, Arthur Balfour, there was a howl of disbelief in the press. It was provoked not by the suspicion of nepotism (who would wish for such a post?) but by the apparent unfitness – in every sense – of the new incumbent. The son of a Scottish laird who had married Lady Blanche Cecil, Balfour was known only as a witty and languid young man, of delicate appearance, who had published a book on philosophy. Anyone less equipped to take on the challenge of Irish nationalism in the late 1880s it would have been hard to imagine, and Parnell's followers exulted: 'We have killed Forster and blinded Beach. What shall we do to Balfour?'

In fact Balfour was physically and intellectually tougher than anyone realised. At Cambridge he had been nicknamed the 'Tiger Lily'; in Ireland he was to earn the soubriquet of 'Bloody Balfour', and he was destined to be the first Chief Secretary to carry out a policy of stern coercion and yet emerge in good health and with an enhanced political reputation. His attitude to the breakdown of law and order in Ireland was summed up in a characteristic aphorism uttered during a debate in the House of Commons: 'There are those who talk as if Irishmen were justified in disobeying the law because the law comes to them in foreign garb. I see no reason why any local colour should be given to the Ten Commandments.'

Irish Nationalist MPs who did not equate the laws

of England with the Ten Commandments had little
[22] difficulty in countering that particular argument, but
in any event it was in the field of actions rather than
words that Irish issues were decided. Armed with the
Criminal Law Amendment Act of 1887, Balfour lost
no time in throwing down the gauntlet to the Irish
National League. This act gave the Lord Lieutenant
powers to suppress any association and to proclaim
any district. If the Crown so wished, a criminal trial
in that district could be moved to another part of the
country and tried not by a 'common' jury but by a
special one with a property qualification. Cases of
intimidation of landlords or tenants, or of taking part
in riots, or of obstructing the police, could be tried
without a jury by two Resident Magistrates.

The legal department in Dublin Castle knew that
if the new legislation was to be administered effectively, a resolute Crown prosecutor would have to be
found. A few days after the act went on the statute
book Edward Carson was appointed counsel to the
Attorney-General for Ireland. He thus, at the age of
thirty-three, found himself in a post which was not
only extremely responsible but downright dangerous,
and which was, in the four years which followed, to
make him known throughout Ireland as 'Coercion
Carson'. It fell to Carson to appear for the Crown in
the first prosecution under the Crimes Act before two
Resident Magistrates. The country round Mitchelstown in Co. Cork had been 'proclaimed' and the
National League suppressed as illegal following the
attempt by the Nationalist MP William O'Brien to
put the 'Plan of Campaign' (a scheme which encouraged the practice of collective bargaining between
tenants and their landlords) into operation on the
estates of the Countess of Kingston. O'Brien and his
colleague John Mandeville were determined to prove
to Balfour the futility of his new policy, and to that

end they addressed two mass meetings of tenants, inciting them to continue the 'Plan'. O'Brien was cer- tain that no witness would dare to come forward with evidence either of the meetings or of what was said. The Attorney-General, however, took up the challenge.

2

The case generated great public excitement, not only in Ireland, but in Britain as well. On 9 September 1887, the day it came on, all the shopkeepers in Mitchelstown closed their premises, while contingents of demonstrators poured in from the surrounding countryside in order to take part in a huge meeting organised in the market square. A party of English Liberal MPs, including Henry Labouchere, arrived to lend their support against coercion, and a number of the Irish MPs also appeared. From early morning vast crowds accompanied by bands had milled about in the streets, which were decorated with flags, green branches, and banners bearing patriotic mottoes. Some men on horseback tried to prevent the police from entering the court.

Carson came into the town from Fermoy, where he had prudently slept the previous night, and he slipped through the dense crowds without difficulty since his distinctive features were still unknown and unrecognised. It was never to be so again. The car-driver was more nervous. 'This is a dangerous business, yer honour,' he said. 'Do you mind if I throw up my cap and say "Three cheers for William O'Brien"?' 'Not in the least,' replied Carson. At the courthouse there was no sign of the prisoners, who did not turn up to surrender their bail and who were in fact addressing the crowd some distance away in the town square. Carson applied to the bench for warrants for their arrest. 'What about a warrant for an MP when the House is

sitting?' one of the magistrates asked nervously. 'It
[24] makes no matter,' Carson told him, and explained the
reasons. The warrants were granted and the court
adjourned.

The police now urged him to leave the court by a
side door, as they could not be responsible for his
safety in the streets after news of the issue of the
warrants had got abroad. Carson refused point-blank.
'The King's highway was made for all, and by that I
will go or not at all,' he said, and immediately went
out on to the courthouse steps. An immense and
sullen crowd was waiting, and as they got a sight of
the execrated 'Castle hack' the shout went up 'To
Hell with Carson!' He stood for a moment calmly
surveying the scene, and then with an enigmatic smile
made his way down the steps. By all the precedents
the enraged mob ought to have knocked him down
and torn him to pieces, but curiosity and incredulity
took over, and perhaps even respect for such reckless
daring. The crowd parted and made way for him. 'Is
it true that you got a warrant for O'Brien's arrest?'
he was asked on all sides. 'I did,' he answered, and
walked unharmed through the streets.[2]

Such rare acts of courage, which a man may respect
in his bitterest enemy, may be foolhardy or carefully
calculated, but they are held to be significant, and not
infrequently they set the seal on greatness. De Gaulle's
greatness was of this kind; so too, in a very different
context, was Carson's. There was also in the incident
something which perhaps only Irishmen can appreci-
ate, something which is vital to understanding Carson's
career and much about Ireland which is puzzling to
outsiders. Like Bernard Shaw, Carson knew well
enough that Ireland is an island entirely surrounded
by footlights. There was perhaps in that smile something which said: 'Come on, boys, you won't harm
me, because I'm as Irish as you are. I know what you

have to do, and you know what I have to do. It's all part of the comedy.'

Yet if it was comedy, it soon, as so often in Ireland, turned to tragedy. Later, as Carson approached the town square, he met people running in every direction, some of them badly injured. By then the square was almost empty except for about forty police drawn up in a line, most of them bleeding and with their uniforms covered in mud, and a shocked John Dillon, who asked Carson if he was the RM. Outside the police barracks a man was lying dead. Carson asked the bystanders to remove the body to the nearest public house, but no one would have anything to do with it. From the carman who had driven him into Mitchelstown that morning Carson learned the full story. While Dillon was addressing the crowd from a wagonette the police had attempted to force a way to the platform for a government reporter who was taking notes for evidence. They were savagely stoned. Reinforcements arrived and were ridden down and trampled by the men on horseback. The policemen retreated as best they could towards the barracks and in self-defence fired a volley, killing three men. Panic ensued, and the huge crowd melted away.

Carson privately thought that the affair had been badly handled. There were too few police, and they had been foolish to try to make a way for the official reporter; he was also contemptuous of the English Liberal MPs for giving their countenance and support to a riot which ended so bloodily. Labouchere had taken refuge in a shop when the firing began, and had hidden under the counter. Carson wrote a hurried report of the events, which eventually reached the Chief Secretary's desk.[3] The incident became known, inevitably, as the Mitchelstown 'massacre', and Gladstone, who was not above this kind of politics, took up the slogan, 'Remember Mitchelstown' and used it against the Conservatives with some effect.

O'Brien's trial began a fortnight later, after he had been arrested and jailed in Cork. This time he arrived in Mitchelstown under heavy military and police escort to the tumultuous cheering of his supporters. The town square was guarded by a troop of hussars with drawn sabres, a company of the Royal Scots Fusiliers with fixed bayonets, and two bodies of police, one armed with rifles. It was only the beginning of a long legal ritual dance between O'Brien and the young prosecutor, in which Carson's stubborn fighting qualities were tested to the full. He had to endure every kind of verbal abuse and was, of course, widely regarded as a Castle hack prepared to do the authorities' legal dirty work for base and unpatriotic motives, money or the hope of office. 'You are', the defence counsel told him in open court, 'low, mean and contemptible, venal and corrupt. You think by this display you will get some position from the Tory government, for whom you are doing this job.' On another occasion the excitable Dr Tanner, a Nationalist MP, threatened him: 'You are a mean ruffianly coward, and I'll take care that before you leave Mitchelstown your head and both your legs will be smashed.'

3

Carson's nerve in face of these onslaughts brought him to Balfour's attention, and he was soon aware that the latter's velvet glove contained an unmistakably iron hand. 'It was Mitchelstown', he concluded, 'that made us certain we had a man at last.' The secret of Balfour's success in Ireland, Carson later asserted, was that he never 'boggled' at anything. 'He simply backed his own people up. After that there wasn't an official in Ireland who didn't worship the ground he walked on.' Soon afterwards Balfour met members of the Irish Bar at a dinner given by the Lord Chancellor. When Carson was introduced to him he said: 'So you are Edward Carson. I am very glad to meet you. There's a great deal I should like to say to you.' And he did say a great deal when the two met again to discuss the problems of enforcing the Crimes Act. Despite their very different backgrounds and intellectual tastes, Balfour seems to have discerned in Carson some affinity of purpose which appealed to him. More immediately, he saw that Carson had exactly the temperament and strength of character needed for the daunting and dangerous work of pacifying the country. Balfour told his niece many years later:

> I made Carson, and he made me. I've told you how no one had courage. Everyone right up to the top was trembling. Some of the RMs were splendid, but on the whole it was an impossible state of affairs. Carson had nerve, however. I sent him all over the place, prosecuting, getting convictions. We worked together.

For his part, Carson showed an admiration for Balfour little short of hero-worship. He told a friend:

> I wish I could give you any notion of the impression he made on me the first time . . . I met him. I was only a provincial lawyer, and, until I saw A. J. B., as he was then, I had never guessed that such an animal could exist. I had never seen anybody like him — nobody in Dublin had.[4]

His friendship with Balfour, which survived some disillusion and disagreement in the next decade, more than any other factor determined the course of his career and brought him into politics. For the moment, however, he *was* only a provincial lawyer, with a stony face and a pronounced Dublin accent, so woebegone in aspect that at least one of his victims (and one who should have known better) was moved to feel pity for him. Wilfrid Scawen Blunt, the eccentric English writer who spent much of his life in the Middle East and who, though Catholic by birth, had fallen under the spell of Islam, had embarked on a one-man crusade against the British Empire. He ardently espoused the cause of Irish nationalism and involved himself in the Plan of Campaign. For addressing an illegal meeting he was tried before two magistrates and sentenced to two weeks' imprisonment. When he appealed against the conviction, Carson and a leading 'silk', John Atkinson, QC, appeared for the Crown. Blunt later wrote that the case against him was conducted by

> two of the Castle bloodhounds, who for high pay did the evil agrarian work in those days for the Government by hunting down the unfortunate peasantry when, in connexion with the eviction campaigns, they came within reach of the law. It was a gloomy role they played, especially Carson's, and I used to feel almost pity for the man when I saw him, as I several times did, thus engaged in the West of Ireland Courts.[5]

It was seldom wise to indulge in pity for Carson when he was in court, particularly when he was hunting down the wealthy, high-born and famous who had transgressed the law. 'I was delighted to see you had run Wilfrid Blunt in,' was Salisbury's unfeeling comment to Balfour. 'The great heart of the people always chuckles when a gentleman gets into the clutches of the law.'

Carson won the case against Blunt, but he lost an even more picturesque one against the Lord Mayor of Dublin, the Rt Hon. T. D. Sullivan, who came to court in his mayoral robes, accompanied by the civic officer carrying the sword and mace, and the entire city council, who tried in vain to take their places in the dock. Sullivan, a well-known nationalist poet and the author of the patriotic song 'God Save Ireland', was prosecuted for publishing a notice of a meeting of the National League in his newspaper, *The Nation*. Brilliantly defended by Tim Healy, he was acquitted on a legal technicality and returned to the Mansion House in triumph. *Punch* celebrated the occasion in light-hearted verse:

> Then up stood Mr Carson, just as quiet as any parson,
> And read out his indictment with a settled stone-
>   like face,
> Till Tim Healy, quick replying, rose then and there
>   denying
> That the Counsel for the Crown had a shadow of a
>   case.

The assiduous Carson did not give up, however, and he took the matter to the High Court. A new trial was ordered, and this time the Lord Mayor was convicted and sent to prison.[6]

But the strain of this work was beginning to tell on Carson, whose health was never good. It involved a great deal of travelling, in circumstances of considerable danger. Annette never knew when he went out in the morning whether he would return to Merrion Square alive. When he travelled up country roads the police searched the hedgerows for assassins. Once a sinister-looking man boarded his train as it was leaving Dublin and crept along the corridor towards his compartment. Carson drew the revolver he always carried and pointed it at the man, who ran away. The whole train was searched, but the suspect had got away undetected. He received threats of every kind: anonymous letters, postcards adorned with a skull and crossbones, and model coffins were sent to him.

He was stoned in the streets. His real ambition was [30] to end his days on the Irish bench, and when a county court judgeship became vacant in 1888 he applied for it to Peter O'Brien, the Attorney-General. 'Peter the Packer' refused point-blank, and in doing so saved him from obscurity. 'The Almighty meant you for bigger things than that,' he told him.[7] In 1889, however, Carson ceased to be the Attorney-General's 'devil' and, again on O'Brien's advice, applied to the Lord Chancellor for leave to take silk. His application was successful in June 1889, and, at thirty-five, he became the youngest QC in the country.

3
The Guiding Star

1

Carson was at last well established in his profession; there was no higher position for him to reach at the Irish Bar, except to become a law officer or a judge. Although an Irish barrister's fees fell short of those earned in England, the cost of living was cheaper in Ireland, and he was now becoming prosperous. As well as the large house in Merrion Square he had a seaside house in Dalkey, where Annette and the children spent the summer months, and Carson such free weekends as he could manage. Harry was at school, the two girls were also growing fast, and in 1890 Annette had another son, Walter Seymour. She was happy, surrounded by her growing family, though she saw less of her husband than ever.

His work was arduous. In addition to his expanding practice, he was still senior Crown prosecutor for Dublin and in charge of all the work at the Green Street court. Ever anxious about his health, Carson looked forward in a few years' time to a less strenuous place on the bench. Balfour had contemplated this prospect with alarm, and in 1890 he had seen an opportunity to make Carson a law officer with a seat in parliament. At that time it seemed likely that the Attorney-General, Serjeant Madden, who was one of the MPs representing Dublin University (i.e. Trinity College), would accept a judicial appointment. Madden postponed his resignation, however, until the general election, which took place in 1892. In the interim

Westminster had been shaken by the O'Shea divorce scandal, the fall of Parnell and his death in October 1891, and the dividing of the Irish Parliamentary Party into bitter factions. When the date of the election was announced in the summer of 1892 Salisbury and Balfour were able to make fresh legal appointments for Ireland. Atkinson replaced Madden as Attorney-General, and Carson was appointed Solicitor-General, being sworn in to his new office on 1 July 1892. He was immediately put forward for the vacant university seat. The only snag was that the Trinity members had always been Tories, and Carson was standing as a Liberal Unionist. Some of the Fellows, who still recalled his undergraduate radicalism, were strongly opposed to him, and they ran a Conservative candidate with an unimpeachable Conservative record, a certain Colonel Lowry. On 9 July the sitting member, David Plunkett, QC, was comfortably re-elected, while Carson took the second seat with 1,609 of the graduates' votes against 897 cast for Lowry.

Making speeches to exuberant Trinity men on the importance of maintaining the Union, and being 'chaired' round the quadrangles by them at high speed, were new and exhausting experiences for Carson. 'Thank God that's all over,' he confided to a friend. 'I'll be staying in parliament for two or three years, then I'll go on the bench at the Four Courts and lead a quiet life.' He could scarcely foresee that thirty years of exacting parliamentary life lay ahead of him before he was allowed to seek that refuge.

The election gave the Gladstonian Liberals and Irish MPs a majority of forty in the new parliament, and it was clear that Carson's term of office as Solicitor-General was destined to be short. The government fell in the debate on the Queen's Speech, and Gladstone, who now became Prime Minister for the fourth time at the age of eighty-three, at once began to prepare a second Home Rule Bill for Ireland. The Home Secretary in the new administration was H. H. Asquith, hardly two years older than Carson, and John Morley returned, after twelve years, as Chief Secretary. His first move on reaching Dublin Castle was to repeal the provisions of the Crimes Act which permitted special inquiries by Resident Magistrates. He also released the men convicted of the murder of a police inspector at Gweedore, Co. Donegal. Undeterred by a bomb outrage which killed a policeman on duty at the Castle, Morley set up a special commission to consider the claims of tenants evicted by their landlords for taking part in the Plan of Campaign, appointing as its president a High Court judge, Sir James Mathew. Mathew, the father-in-law of John Dillon, and a nephew of the renowned Capuchin apostle of temperance, Father Mathew,[1] was an ardent Home Ruler. He made no secret of his partisan sympathy with the tenants and soon showed that he was prepared to set aside the rules of judicial procedure on their behalf.

This attitude brought him into sensational conflict with Carson on the very first day of the commission's sitting. Carson had been briefed to appear for a number of landlords, including Lord Clanrickarde, who was perhaps the most hated landowner in Ireland. The trouble began when Mathew refused to allow Carson to cross-examine John Roche, the MP for East Galway, who had organised the Plan of Campaign on the Clanrickarde estate. 'My Lord,' said Carson very slowly and deliberately, 'if I am not at liberty to cross-examine, I say the whole thing is a farce and a sham. I willingly withdraw from it. I will not prostitute my position by remaining any longer as an advocate before an English judge.'

'I am not sitting as a judge,' barked Mathew.

'Any fool could see that,' muttered Carson under

his breath, but loud enough to be heard by everyone
in the room.

The president was furious. 'Your observations are disgraceful,' he said. William O'Brien, who was present, shouted at Carson: 'You are not in a coercion court now.' Another counsel, William Kenny, QC, joined Carson in protest, only to come in his turn under the lash of Mr Justice Mathew's tongue. At this Carson flung his papers down on the table and walked out of the room with the other counsel following.

It was the kind of histrionic gesture for which he was to become famous, or even notorious, and it created a sensation on both sides of the Irish Sea. He was both praised and attacked, and he defended his conduct in the columns of *The Times*. On the whole his action was supported by the public as well as by his colleagues. Two of the commissioners resigned, and the landlords as a body refused to take any further part in its proceedings. This was Carson's last professional appearance in Ireland. As soon as it had become clear that he would need to be constantly at Westminster to advise Balfour on Irish affairs, he began to consider giving up his practice at the Irish Bar and trying to find legal work in England. It was a calculated risk, for no barrister he knew of had abandoned his Irish practice and made good at the English Bar. Moreover Carson was, as he was soon to betray, quite unfamiliar with the procedures of the Temple, which were so different from those of the Four Courts. But once again he was exceptionally fortunate.

At the Carlton Club, of which he had just become a member, he was introduced to Charles Darling, QC, who was later to become a famous judge. 'I suppose you have come here to take the bread out of our mouths?' Darling asked him. 'No', replied Carson, 'but I daresay I'll have a desk in the library.' Darling was puzzled at first by this allusion, but soon realised that the young Irishman, in spite of having risen to the position of Irish Solicitor-General, was totally un- familiar with practice at the English Bar. He explained that several barristers joined together in the same chambers, sharing the services of a clerk. 'It'll be no use my taking chambers here,' said Carson in his usual doleful way. 'I'll be no one, and nobody'll know me.'

Darling disagreed. The prosecutions which Carson had conducted under the Crimes Act in Ireland had been widely reported in the English newspapers, and his name was known in legal circles. 'Look here, Carson,' said Darling, intrigued by the Irishman's pessimism, 'I'll tell you what. You let me paint your name up outside my chambers, and you'll have five times my practice inside a year.'

'I know I won't, but I'll bet you a shilling.'

'Done!' said Darling.

So it was arranged that when Carson was called to the English Bar he would join Darling in his chambers at No. 3 Dr Johnson's Buildings in the Temple. This was the foundation of Carson's career in the English courts.[2]

2

As Leader of the Opposition in the Commons in the new parliament Balfour sent for Carson to brief him on the suspension of the Crimes Act provisions, the release of the Gweedore prisoners and the doings of the Evicted Tenants Commission. The new session of parliament opened on 31 January 1893. Balfour was to open the debate on the Address to the Queen's Speech, and he planned to put up Carson to give a detailed reply to Morley, who was expected to speak towards the end of the debate. These were formidable circumstances in which to make a maiden speech — it was believed to be the first time such a speech had been delivered from the Opposition front bench — but

they were made more daunting by the excited atmos-
[36] phere of the House on the third day of the debate,
2 February. Morley was not called on by the Speaker
until 10 p.m., and as it was then customary for the
debate to go on until midnight, there seemed at first
ample time for Carson to reply. But Morley, who was
frequently interrupted, did not resume his seat until
11.30, and all this time Carson was enduring an agony
of nerves. With only half an hour in which to reply,
he asked Balfour if it would not be better to adjourn
until the next day instead of making his speech in two
parts. The motion for adjournment was put to a division by the government, however, and defeated. This
occupied fifteen minutes, and when Carson rose to his
feet, the hands on the clock above the Speaker's chair
pointed to a quarter to twelve.

It is a convention of the House of Commons that a
maiden speech should be heard without interruption.
Carson was nevertheless certain that the Nationalist
MPs would give him a rough time. He was extremely
nervous, though as usual he strove to conceal his ner-
vousness. His courtroom experience was of limited
help, since the atmosphere of the House of Commons
was so very different. When the jeers and catcalls died
away below the gangway he began to speak quietly in
his distinctive Dublin accent. He made obeisance to
the House and its procedure, but said he thought
adjournment a reasonable suggestion. Nevertheless,
he began, against the clock, to examine Morley's six
months in office. The House had become very quiet
and attentive, anxious to hear how this new Irish MP
would perform. The Irish were usually reliable enter-
tainers. From time to time he turned round to Balfour,
as if for encouragement. He had begun with Morley's
claim that there had been a fall in agrarian crime,
arguing that it was because no criminals had been
brought to justice, and then he turned to the boast

that rents were being paid better than ever. 'It is certainly a curious coincidence that in the year when there is this great agricultural depression we should find the Chief Secretary for Ireland boasting that rents are particularly well paid in Ireland.' As he spoke these words Big Ben began to chime midnight, the Speaker called 'Order, order,' and the debate stood adjourned.

Carson, unaware of the good impression created by his opening remarks, went home in a mood of the blackest pessimism. He hardly slept, and when a friend called on him next morning he found him still in bed, complaining that he was ill and had failed miserably. He hoped somehow to be able to drag himself to the House and hurry through the rest of his speech as best he could. When he arrived there some time later he had once more to endure long hours of waiting while writs were moved for new elections in constituencies (mostly Irish) where returns had been declared void. It was growing dusk, and the gas lamps were lighted, before he again got up before the dispatch box. The torture of waiting had added an edge to his Irish temper. He lashed the Evicted Tenants Commission and its president, who had refused him the right of cross-examination. He could tell the House of Commons what he had not been able to refer to in court, that Roche had incited Clanrickarde's tenants to attack his land agent, as a result of which the agent's body was soon afterwards discovered riddled with bullets, and that Roche had stated that he had helped to resist the sheriff at an eviction. At this point Roche, who had hurried back into the chamber, interrupted to say he was proud to have been present at the eviction. 'Exactly,' said Carson. 'I make no charge against the honourable Member. I am not accusing him of resisting the eviction, but having regard to the fact that he was there and proud of it, I suggest that at least I was entitled to put one question in cross-examination.'

There was some laughter, and Carson began to feel more confident. Roche, he said, had made another speech exhorting the tenants of a landlord named Lewis to throttle him 'until the glass eye fell out of his head'. Again Roche leapt to his feet. 'I did not tell the tenantry to throttle him,' he protested, 'but I admit that in the heat and excitement of the moment ... I did make use of the expression that by adhering loyally to their pledges they would throttle him, and I hoped they would not loose their grip until the glass eye fell out of his head.' This time the laughter was general, and Carson, relaxed now, turned to other matters. When he sat down he had been speaking for more than an hour, and though it was past the usual time for dining, the House remained full. To his astonishment the speech was greeted by cheering which lasted for several minutes. Balfour patted him on the back, and MPs crowded round him in the lobby with their congratulations. On the government front bench Asquith gave an approving nod — mercifully the gift of seeing into the future was denied him — and Gladstone said that it was the best maiden speech he remembered. That night as Joseph Chamberlain drove away from the House he told his son Austen: 'A new force has arisen in politics.' It was fortunate that Austen Chamberlain, too, could not see into the future.[3]

3

Carson awoke next morning to find himself a celebrity. *The Times* devoted a leader to his speech, and the Liberal *Pall Mall Gazette* conceded that the Opposition had secured a redoubtable ally. Even the *Tailor's Gazette* praised the cut of his frock-coat. The press described his tallness, his distinctive appearance, his brooding melancholy countenance, his Irish accent, his smile, his repartee. Much of the press's relish resulted, of course, from the satisfaction of seeing how an Irish- man could treat other Irishmen to a strong dose of their own medicine. As George III said, if you want to baste an Irishman, you can easily get an Irishman to turn the spit. Overnight, on the eve of his thirty-ninth birthday, Carson had achieved an impressive parliamentary reputation. But sweet though the triumph was, the way ahead was still unclear. Annette and the children were not with him in London to share the hour; they had to be maintained in Dublin, and his savings were rapidly diminishing. He had taken a set of furnished rooms at No. 19 Bury Street, off St James's Street, not too far from the House or the Carlton Club. Life in London was expensive, and there seemed little hope of legal work. He was not called to the English Bar at the Middle Temple until 26 April 1893.

His first English case was a suit in chancery, brought to him in an unusual way by a solicitor who called on him at the House of Commons. Then one or two briefs began to come in to No. 3 Dr Johnson's Buildings. Although he was an Irish QC, Carson was rated as a junior at the English Bar, and this was the cause of much confusion when he was 'leading' in a case. His first big case came within three months, a libel action brought against the *Evening News* by a Liberal MP and trade union leader, J. H. Wilson. Carson appeared for the newspaper. His cross-examination of Wilson was devastating, revealing a pathetic story of financial incompetence, and in the end the plaintiff was led away from the courtroom weeping and sobbing. Carson won his case without producing a single witness. It was a signal triumph, displaying his great strength in cross-examination which one QC described as superior to that of the acknowledged leaders of the Bar at the time, Sir Charles Russell and Sir Edward Clarke. What

touched Carson most, though, was a telegram of congratulations from his old colleagues in the Four Courts
in Dublin.

While building up his practice in the English courts
Carson was fully occupied with his duties in parliament. He had to live up to the reputation he had won
with his maiden speech. But it was in the long and
tedious debates over the second Home Rule Bill that
he enhanced that reputation and made it secure.

The principal driving force behind the bill was
Gladstone himself, whose fourth and final premier-
ship lasted from 15 August 1892 until 3 March 1894.
His energy was remarkable for a man who was already
in his eighty-fourth year when he took office, but inevitably his leadership had lost some of its earlier drive.
One motive still impelled him, a duty to try once
again to give Ireland self-government. He introduced
his second Home Rule Bill in February 1893. It differed from that of 1886 in providing for Irish repre-
sentation at Westminster, but once again made no
reference to the opposition to Home Rule of the
Northern Protestants. They, for their part, had already
closed their ranks and organised a formidable resistance movement. As early as June 1892, some weeks
before the general election and the widely expected
Liberal victory, the Ulster Unionists had held a huge
convention in Belfast at which they solemnly swore
that 'We will not have Home Rule.' In the following
months their cause was taken up by prominent British Conservatives, notably Salisbury and Balfour, both
of whom travelled to Ireland to address Unionist
rallies. Against this background of rising excitement
in Ireland, the debates at Westminster dragged on inter-
minably, eventually occupying over two hundred
hours of parliament's time.

Night after night in the hot summer of 1893 Carson
sat vigilant on the Opposition front bench, ready to

rebut this or that argument of the government or its Irish allies. In these months he perfected his parlia- mentary style, which was never elegant nor eloquent, but usually effective. His opponents were his mentors, Harcourt, Morley, Asquith, Healy, Dillon, Redmond and, of course, the great Gladstone himself. Yet he never managed to shake off the habits acquired as Crown prosecutor. As the parliamentary correspondent of *Punch* commented,

> When he is discussing the speech or action of an hon. or right hon. gentleman opposite, he always treats him as if he had found him in the dock, and as if his brief hinted at unutterable crimes brought home by the inquiry and testimony of members of the Irish Constabulary. The manner is so natural and ingrained that there is doubt whether it will be overcome or even modified. This is a pity for it is simply professional. Nevertheless — indeed, therefore — it will never do in the House of Commons.[4]

Carson *did* modify this characteristic in later years, but, like so many lawyers in the Commons, he never quite lost the mark of the advocate.

At the conclusion of the committee stage of the bill an extraordinary scene took place when a shouting match between Carson and some of the Liberal MPs led to a general fracas. The MP for Market Harborough, J. W. Logan, sat down in a threatening attitude beside Carson on the Opposition front bench, but before he could strike him, a quiet and respectable member sitting behind Carson caught Logan under the chin and pulled his head back over the bench. The Irish Nationalist MPs immediately joined in, trying to attack the redoubtable and outspoken Colonel Saunderson, the leader of the small unattached group of Ulster Unionist MPs. Dr Tanner approached him from behind and struck him on his bald head, whereupon Saunderson turned round and sent him flying [42] with a sweep of his long arm. Soon fighting was going on in every part of the chamber, and the outraged spectators in the galleries began to hiss. The Speaker was sent for (a deputy had been in the chair), and he surveyed the scene sternly like a schoolmaster returning to a neglected classroom. When at last the scuffling ceased, Gladstone stood up and apologised for the House, an embarrassed senior pupil who had failed to keep order in the master's absence.

Such scenes were always possible when Ireland and her woes were under discussion, and Carson could not foresee that worse would occur in time and that he would be the central figure in them. For the present the Home Rule Bill passed its third reading by thirty-four votes, but was at once thrown out by the House of Lords on 8 September 1893. It was a disappointment for Gladstone, who had hoped to see it on the statute book before he retired, but it was not an unexpected one. The Tory House of Lords was still the bulwark of the Union, and for as long as the Tories set their face against Home Rule the Union was safe.

But would they always do so? At the end of his first arduous session of parliament Carson found himself at some non-political gathering in conversation with Sir William Harcourt, the Liberal Chancellor of the Exchequer.

'You're a young man, full of enthusiasm for your cause, are you not?' asked Harcourt.

'Yes,' said Carson. 'And you put absolute trust in your party,' continued Harcourt. 'I can see that.'

'Yes,' said Carson.

'Well, sir,' said Harcourt, 'sooner or later there is going to be a terrible disillusion for you. The Conservatives, mark my word, never yet took up a cause without betraying it in the end, and I don't think you'll betray it with them.'[5]

Carson's star was now in the ascendant. In November [43] 1893 he received the coveted accolade of a cartoon by 'Spy' in *Vanity Fair*, an honour which had recently been accorded to Oscar Wilde. The cartoon was accompanied by a brief biography from the satirical pen of 'Jehu Junior' which recorded that

> He contrives, though he has not yet made a great name as a statesman, to say even more distasteful things about the oppressed Nationalists than the most brutal of Saxons. He is a bold and sinuous person, who pays no heed at all to the persuasions of the Nationalists who so prettily chide him for his want of patriotism. He seems to like the disgrace of being stigmatised as Mr Balfour's Crown Prosecutor; nor is he put out when he is openly said to be as big a blackguard as ever was Peter the Packer.... Yet he is not without virtue. He has not much practice in England; but he has appeared in a case which arose out of a modern Labour trouble, and it is possible he will get more clients. For he is a hard-working, painstaking, lynx-eyed practitioner who can speak strongly. He is a lean, pale-faced Irishman, who has as much wit and ability as Irishmen often have. He has not fattened even on robust Unionism.[6]

In truth Carson's English practice was growing very rapidly, and in the spring of 1894 Darling reminded him of their bet. His clerk had been going through Carson's fee book and found that Carson's practice was indeed five times Darling's. A few days later Carson presented Darling with an Irish blackthorn walking-stick that had cost exactly a shilling. It had a silver band with the inscription 'C. D. from E. C. 1894'. In the same year Carson applied to the Lord Chancellor, Lord Herschell, to become a [44] QC at the English Bar. Herschell replied that there was no precedent for creating a QC of scarcely a year's standing at the English Bar, even if he was already an Irish 'silk' and former Solicitor-General for Ireland, and that he would have to wait the regulation nine-year period for qualification. The snub infuriated Carson. It was not only a personal insult; he considered it an affront to the entire Irish Bar, and he vowed never to renew his application while Herschell remained Lord Chancellor. Politics provided the explanation, for the Liberals had seized on this pretext for a petty revenge on him because of his attacks on Morley and the Evicted Tenants Commission. Others took up his cause — the grateful *Evening News* and Sir Henry Hawkins, the judge who had sponsored his application — and Herschell at last relented, agreeing to create an additional QC for that year on condition that Carson accepted the patent from his hands. Carson swallowed his pride and did so, but though both men punctiliously observed every detail of the ceremony, appearing in full dress of full-bottomed wig, knee-breeches and buckled shoes, they exchanged not a single word, and Carson strode away, without even the customary handshake and congratulations, to be called 'within the Bar' by the judges presiding in each court. It was the first time that an Irish QC had ever 'taken silk' in England.

No one was more pleased by Carson's success than his friends Lord and Lady Londonderry. They had followed his progress with keen interest since their viceregal days in Dublin, and Carson for his part was grateful for their influential friendship in England. Of Lord Londonderry he said: 'When I came over here, if he had been my own brother he could not have been kinder.' Londonderry House, the mansion in Park Lane where Lady Londonderry entertained on the grand scale, and to which the leading figures of the day coveted invitations, became for Carson a second home. He was frequently a guest, too, at Mount Stewart in Co. Down and Wynyard Park in Co. Durham, their magnificent country residences. Carson in the days of his later fame speculated on whether his biographer would ever really understand how pleasant his visits to Mount Stewart and Wynyard Park had been, and why Lord and Lady Londonderry had always been so kind to him.

Lady Londonderry often watched the debates in the House of Commons from behind the grille above the press gallery, the only place from which ladies were, in those days, allowed to view the MPs at work, and she seems to have derived genuine pleasure from the parliamentary achievements of her protégé, 'the Solicitor' as she always called him, in allusion to his first office. It was to her he was to confide all his problems and anxieties, public and private, over the next three decades. Through her salon at Londonderry House she exercised a considerable influence in the counsels of the Conservative Party, and she was a political ally of some importance.

The ablest advocate then at the English Bar, and the only one Carson feared, was another Irishman, the Attorney-General Sir Charles Russell. In the same month that Carson 'took silk' Russell went to the House of Lords as a Lord of Appeal, with the title of Lord Russell of Killowen, and a few weeks later he was to become Lord Chief Justice. 'Exit one Irishman, enter another,' reported one of the newspapers. 'Sir Charles Russell will no longer plead a cause, and his place looks like being taken by Mr Carson.' By an odd coincidence Russell's son, a solicitor, now brought to Carson the famous and tragic case which was to put him at one bound into the front rank of English advocates.

A month or two earlier Carson had been crossing

the Strand one day when he was almost knocked down
[46] by a fine carriage drawn by two horses. The carriage
stopped, and out stepped Carson's old college contemporary, Oscar Wilde. Wilde was at the very height of
his fame as a playwright and a literary lion in London
society, one whose witticisms were attentively gathered and repeated in drawing-rooms throughout the
country. He had become plump and prosperous; his
countenance bore all the marks of high living and self-
indulgence, and he was flamboyantly attired, ex-
hibiting a white carnation in his button-hole. 'Hullo,
Ned Carson, how are you?' he said affably, stretching
out his hand, which Carson shook. 'Fancy you being
a Tory and Arthur Balfour's right-hand man! You're
coming along, Ned. Come and dine with me one day
in Tite Street.' Carson had never liked Wilde, but he
was touched by his friendliness. Had he accepted the
invitation, Wilde's tragic history might have been different, for it was Carson's strict rule never to appear
against anyone from whom he had accepted hospital-
ity. The brief which Russell now offered him was to
defend the Marquess of Queensberry against a charge
of criminal libel, and the prosecution had been initiated by Wilde.

Queensberry, who is remembered as the author of
the rules which govern boxing, was an ill-natured
Scottish peer of eccentric opinions. He had been a
tyrant to his family, alienating his sensitive and beautiful wife by his abominable behaviour, and quarrelling
bitterly with his sons. His third son, Lord Alfred
Douglas, had fallen under Wilde's spell while still an
undergraduate at Oxford. He had some ability as a
poet and as an athlete, and Wilde was attracted to him
also because of his good looks and his aristocratic con-
nections. The ecstatic letters which he wrote to Douglas, containing sentences like 'It is a marvel that those
red rose-leaf lips of yours should have been made no

less for the music of song than for madness of kisses,' unluckily found their way into the hands first of a would-be blackmailer and then of Queensberry. Like everyone else, Queensberry had heard the rumours that were circulating about Wilde, and he was infuriated that his son's name should be linked with him in this way. After a series of provocations, including threats of horse-whipping and an attempt to disrupt the first night of *The Importance of Being Earnest*, he brought matters to a head by leaving a card at Wilde's club, on which he had written: 'To Oscar Wilde, posing as a sodomite'.

It was a cunning taunt, for he calculated that the words 'posing as' would make a libel difficult to prove. However, when Wilde discovered the card ten days later he at once consulted his solicitor, and next day Queensberry was arrested on a charge of criminal libel. Carson at first refused the brief on the grounds of his acquaintance with the prosecutor, but eventually, after hearing more of the evidence which Russell had collected and having consulted Lord Halsbury, a former Lord Chancellor, he decided to take the defence. A private detective employed by Queensberry had established that the rooms of a young man called Taylor were at the centre of an extensive homosexual circle, and that Wilde had visited them, though there was no evidence to link him criminally with any of the men concerned. At the last moment, however, Russell succeeded in tracking down a valet named Parker who was prepared to admit to having had homosexual relations with Wilde at the Savoy Hotel. Until then Carson had been inclined to advise Queensberry to plead guilty, but armed with this evidence he prepared to fight the prosecution all the way.

The celebrity of the parties involved ensured that the case received the most sensational publicity, and the court was packed to capacity when the case opened on 3 April 1895, though no women cared to [48] be seen in the galleries. Sir Edward Clarke, the outstanding advocate of the day, a short rotund figure with a deceptively benign countenance like a country parson, opened for the prosecution. It was a daunting performance for Carson to hear. 'I never heard anything to equal it in all my life,' he admitted. Wilde took the stand brimful of confidence and answered his counsel's questions with easy assurance, but when he gave his age as thirty-nine Carson suddenly sat up and made a note. When Wilde had first learned that Carson was to cross-examine him he said: 'Then I am sure that he will do so with all the added bitterness of an old friend;' but really he was certain he had nothing to fear from the experience. He remembered Carson at Trinity, plodding along when Wilde was sweeping off every prize in sight. He knew Carson's mind and how it operated, the plainness of his speech, still with its strong Dublin twang, and the dogged harsh logic of his argument. He was fatally tempted to use Carson's questions as targets for the swift and glittering arrows of his unsurpassed wit.

When Carson rose to cross-examine, his very first question revealed how much Wilde had underestimated his courtroom skill. 'You stated that your age was thirty-nine. I think you are over forty? You were born on 16th October 1854?' Wilde had been detected in a stupid and unnecessary lie and stood revealed to the jury as a man vain about his age. He showed no discomfiture, however, and went on to entertain the court with his quick-witted replies to Carson's deliberate questions. Asked if he thought a certain publication was not immoral, Wilde replied: 'It was worse — it was badly written.' Soon the court was in gales of laughter, and all of it against Carson, who did not appear to be taking it well. He became ever paler than usual, and beads of perspiration appeared on his forehead. He read out one of the letters to Lord Alfred Douglas: 'Your slim gilt soul walks between passion and poetry.' He read it again in such a way as to make it clear to the jury just what he thought of it. 'Is that a beautiful phrase?' he asked Wilde. 'Not as you read it, Mr Carson. You read it very badly.' Carson almost lost his temper. Some of these cuts were deeper than the audience could divine; old sensitivities were being irritated. The court gradually came to realise the deadly nature of the duel between these two.

Doggedly, Carson read through the letters, as he had earlier read through extracts from Wilde's published work. 'Is that an ordinary letter?' 'Everything I write is extraordinary. I do not pose as being ordinary. Great Heavens, ask me any question you like about it.' But Carson asked him only one question: 'Is it the kind of letter a man writes to another?' Carson then turned to the names of the young men mentioned in the plea of justification. Had Wilde not given this one and that one expensive presents? He produced a signed photograph of Wilde, a cigarette case and a silver-mounted walking-stick. Had he not bought this boy a suit of blue serge and a straw hat with a band of red and blue? 'That, I think, was his own unfortunate selection,' was Wilde's riposte. There was less laughter now. The jury began to look solemn. Wilde lost some of his confidence.

The next morning, as he took his place in the witness box, he seemed more subdued. However, his wit was as keen as ever. Carson questioned him closely about the valet Parker and his brother, a groom. Why had Wilde given them expensive dinners and iced champagne? Did he drink champagne himself? 'Yes,' said Wilde. 'Iced champagne is a favourite drink of mine – strongly against my doctor's orders.' 'Never mind your doctor's orders, sir,' rasped Carson. 'I never do,' said Wilde, and the court was convulsed with

laughter. Carson was now leading Wilde on to very
[50] dangerous ground; the questions were detailed and
particular, and Sir Edward Clarke was becoming distinctly uneasy. All these grooms and valets and un-
employed youths who were not artists and had no
interest in literature, what had they to offer a man
like Wilde in return for his generosity to them? Then
Carson sprang his surprise, a letter from Parker.
Clarke asked to see the handwriting. Carson put on
his grimmest expression. 'Parker himself will be here,
which is better.' This produced a sensation in court,
since Parker had been offered no immunity and must
therefore be willing to incriminate himself. The climax
of this remarkable cross-examination was reached
when Carson asked Wilde about a boy called Grainger,
who was Lord Alfred Douglas's servant in Oxford.
'Did you kiss him?' Carson asked. For one fatal moment Wilde's quick wits deserted him. 'Oh dear, no,' he
replied without thinking. 'He was a peculiarly plain
boy. He was, unfortunately, extremely ugly. I pitied
him for it.' Carson pounced like a tiger. Was that the
reason Wilde had never kissed him? Suddenly Wilde
was on the verge of breaking down. 'Oh, Mr Carson,
you are pertinently insolent.' But Carson continued
his remorseless questions. 'You sting me and insult
me and try to unnerve me, and at times one says
things flippantly when one ought to speak more seriously. I admit it.' At this Carson gathered together
his papers and sat down.

Clarke quickly tried to repair the damage in his
re-examination, but it was too late. When the court
reassembled after lunch Wilde was not in his place,
and at first the rumour spread round the Old Bailey
that he had fled rather than face Carson again. But
fifteen minutes later Wilde appeared, apologising to
the bench because the clock in the restaurant where
he had lunched was slow. Carson did not ask to cross-

examine further, but began his opening speech for his client. He said that he proposed to put into the wit- ness-box the young men with whom Wilde had associated and the hotel staff. 'The wonder is not that the gossip reached Lord Queensberry,' he declared, 'but that, after it was known, this man Wilde should have been tolerated in society in London for the length of time he has.' A short time later Sir Edward Clarke, who had briefly left the court, returned and began to pluck at Carson's gown. He whispered in his ear that he had consulted his client and that his instructions were now to withdraw from the prosecution. It was all over. Clarke addressed the judge. What had been admitted might well induce the jury to say that Lord Queensberry was justified in using the word 'posing'. If the case were to continue, he could not expect a verdict for his client and 'we should be going through, day after day, investigation of matters of the most appalling character'. In these circumstances he was prepared to accept a verdict of not guilty in reference to the word 'posing'.

The jury brought in a verdict of not guilty, and Queensberry was immediately released. Two hours later Wilde was arrested at the Cadogan Hotel and sent for trial. The sun-god had fallen abruptly to earth, humbled by the plodding contemporary he had tried to patronise. Ahead of him lay only ruin, shame, imprisonment and exile. Meanwhile congratulations poured in on Carson. The judge took a sheet of court writing paper and scribbled:

Dear Carson,

I never heard a more powerful speech or a more searching cross-examination.

I congratulate you on having escaped most of the filth.

In truth Carson, while conscious of his triumph, had

no feeling of elation. Never sanctimonious or fond of
moral censure, he hated the part he had to play, and
even went to the Solicitor-General to ask: 'Cannot
you let up on the fellow now? He has suffered a great
deal.' But, as the Solicitor-General pointed out, the
case could not be dropped lest it be said abroad that
it had been covered up because of some of the names
mentioned. Wilde was given the maximum sentence
of two years' imprisonment, during which he wrote
his best-remembered poem, *The Ballad of Reading
Gaol*. On his release, disgraced and financially ruined,
he went to live in Paris and died there three years
later.[7]

5

At the general election of 1895 the Conservatives were
returned with a majority of 133. Salisbury again
became Prime Minister with Balfour as First Lord of the
Treasury and Leader of the House. Carson seemed to
have an excellent chance of becoming either Solicitor-
General or Attorney-General in the new government,
but strictly speaking he was still an outsider and he
was passed over in favour of two leading lights of the
English Bar. By now, however, he was the senior MP
for Dublin University — his new colleague was the
historian W. E. H. Lecky — and this meant that by
tradition he became a member of the Irish Privy Council and was entitled to the style of 'Right Honourable'.

Early in the new parliament a serious difference
developed between Carson and his hero Balfour over
the Irish Land Bill, introduced by Arthur's brother
Gerald, the Irish Chief Secretary. In furtherance of
the Tory policy of 'killing Home Rule by kindness',
Gerald Balfour hoped to remove some of the Nationalist grievances by giving yet more advantages to tenants.
Carson considered this a betrayal of the landlords, and
indirectly of Unionism. From Joseph Chamberlain's

old seat on the backbenches he inveighed bitterly
against his friends, accusing them of going back on
their words. At the height of the quarrel he stalked
out of the House, followed by Colonel Saunderson
and other Unionist stalwarts. Carson enjoyed this kind
of melodrama, but he believed that his action was
fully justified. He never came to terms with the English
politician's easy withdrawal from principles once
professed. He could not learn that when a minister
said 'black' in the House of Commons he really meant
'white'. Nor could he play the party game of attacking
unpopular policies in Opposition and then adopting
them when in government.

Balfour, though undoubtedly nettled, was too
urbane to allow the rift to become permanent. Carson,
he reported to Queen Victoria,

> is a man of great ability, and has a somewhat bitter
> tongue. He made a speech to which Mr Balfour
> thought it necessary to make a strong reply. But no
> permanent breach has, or will, result; which is a
> source of great gratification to Mr Balfour, as he has
> a great admiration and regard for Mr Carson, who
> served under him as Solicitor-General for Ireland
> through many difficult times.[8]

These were bland phrases, but wounding things had
been said on both sides, and for a while there *was* a
public breach in Balfour's relations with Carson,
who renounced the party whip and declared: 'Hence-
forward I am resolved to take whatever course is best
for Ireland.'

Carson's omission from the government, however
disappointing it may have been, proved of great professional advantage to him. For five years he was free to
build up his private practice, and in that time he became one of the leading advocates in the country,
acclaimed as a successor to Russell and compared with

the great counsel of the day. Briefs now began to pour
into Dr Johnson's Buildings, though not more than
half of them were accepted, for Carson, unlike some
other counsel, would take only one case at a time. It
was the clerk and not the principal who decided the
fees, and to Carson's astonishment the sum marked
on the briefs went on increasing at a phenomenal
rate. He was not greedy about fees, and sometimes
asked his clerk, Mr Herepath, to reduce them, but the
pace was set by his growing rivalry with Rufus Isaacs,
the able young QC against whom he found himself
more and more frequently appearing. 'In future',
Herepath told him, 'I propose to tell solicitors that
your fee is the same as Mr Isaacs'.' The fees went up
and up until Isaacs' clerk had the nerve to ask for five
hundred guineas. Herepath then insisted on the same.
The solicitor concerned protested strongly, and even
insisted on seeing Carson personally, but in the end
he paid the fee, and Carson won the case.

One winter afternoon a visitor knocked at the door
of Carson's chambers. He spoke with a pronounced
Irish accent and gave his name as O'Brien. The London
clerk, terrified, almost slammed the door in his face.
This was surely the agitator that Carson had once sent
to jail! Visions of an Irish political murder arose
before his eyes. It was all Mr Darling's fault for bringing an Irishman into chambers. Sensing the hostility,
the stranger produced his card, and the clerk read on
it: 'Lord O'Brien of Kilfenora, Kildare Street Club,
Dublin'. It was Peter the Packer himself, now Lord
Chief Justice of Ireland. Shown into Carson's room,
he gazed around at a sea of white paper and pink tape
and reflected with satisfaction how in 1888 he had
saved Carson from the Irish county court bench.[9]

In 1896 Carson was led by Sir Edward Clarke in one
of the greatest state trials of British history, that in
which Dr Leander Starr Jameson, the leader of the

disastrous 'Jameson Raid' into the Transvaal, was arraigned for the offence of conducting a warlike expedition from British territory against a country with which Great Britain was on friendly terms. Despite great public sympathy for the prisoners, and a jury reluctant to convict, Jameson and his friends were at length found guilty and imprisoned. It was one of the few cases in which Carson found himself on the losing side, and it was not without irony in the light of Carson's own role in Ulster some sixteen years later. But it was followed by a whole series of actions in which Carson was the victorious leading counsel.

These were years of great prosperity for Carson. In 1899 his fees gave him an income of £20,000, a huge sum in the days when the pound had its value and income tax was negligible, and in the same year he turned away briefs valued at £30,000. Suddenly he was a rich man. His entire lifestyle had changed. The bedsitting room in Bury Street was replaced by a fine mansion in Rutland Gate and a country house in the village of Rottingdean. There he met Sir Edward Burne-Jones the artist and his son Philip, who was to paint his portrait, and through them Stanley Baldwin and his famous cousin Rudyard Kipling. Annette had left Dublin with reluctance; she was never happy in London, despite their new wealth and social position. Carson's success and his sudden transformation into a public figure made her bewildered and apprehensive. The couple were no longer happy as they had been in the dangerous days of struggle and poverty in Dublin. Carson had even less time to spend with his family, and already his son Harry was causing him worry. All this contributed to a deepening melancholy and pessimism in Carson's personality.

Politically, he was still in the wilderness, intervening in debates to speak only on Irish questions. On one of these he even opposed his former Unionist

friends and sided with the Nationalists by enthusiastic-
[56] ally supporting the project for the establishment of
a Catholic university in Ireland. (This was in effect
achieved in 1908 with the establishment of the
National University of Ireland by the Liberal government of Sir Henry Campbell-Bannerman.) He was to
remain a consistent supporter of the Catholic claims,
and he was to stick to the cause even when in office,
in defiance of governmental policy.

4
Sir Edward

1

In 1900 Balfour sent for his recalcitrant disciple once
more and, to Carson's surprise, asked him if he would
accept the office of Solicitor-General of England.
Lord Salisbury, he told him, was very anxious that he
should.[1] Carson hesitated. To become a law officer
again (the salary was £6,000 a year) meant a considerable financial sacrifice, and many of his colleagues
urged him to stay at the Bar and become 'the greatest
and richest advocate of our time'. In the end, however, he accepted. The selection of a Tory 'rebel'
over the head of loyal and conscientious lawyers who
had faithfully served the party caused some heartburn-
ing, and the Liberal *Westminster Gazette* published a
cartoon which showed Salisbury as headmaster of a
school awarding the prize to the 'Naughty Big Boy'
while the 'Good Little Boy' (Alfred Cripps, QC) was
passed over. Thus Carson attained the unique distinction of having been successively Solicitor-General of
Ireland and of England. Other honours accompanied
the appointment. He was knighted (by the Prince of
Wales, as the Queen was now old and ill) and the
Middle Temple, at which Inn of Court he had been
called, elected him a bencher. He was forty-six years
of age.

He threw himself into the work with such dedication that by the end of the year he had undermined
his health. In January 1901 Queen Victoria's long
reign drew to a close, and Carson, unwell and in great

pain from severe neuralgia in his side, struggled to his [58] place in the House of Commons as the members swore allegiance to the new monarch, Edward VII. As soon as the ceremony was over he went to his doctor, who ordered a complete rest for several weeks. Carson at once wrote to Balfour, offering to resign if his illness was likely to cause the government inconvenience, but Balfour would not hear of it. 'I have felt for some time past', he wrote, 'that you were perhaps overdoing yourself, and it would really be criminal folly not to take every precaution while there is yet time. I hope soon to welcome you back completely restored.'

Fortunately he did recover quickly, and with undiminished vigour appeared for the Crown in a number of sensational trials. The first was the trial of Earl Russell for bigamy before the House of Lords. The law said that a peer of the realm charged with any felony must be tried by his peers, and so the case was also a rare and picturesque historical occasion. (Such a trial is described fictionally by Dorothy L. Sayers in her detective novel *Clouds of Witness*.) Lord Russell (unlike Miss Sayers's Duke of Denver) was found guilty, but he lived to obtain a free pardon in 1911 and subsequently to hold high office in the state. The important case of *Rex v. Krause* in 1902 became an authority for the proposition in law that where an accused is charged with soliciting one person to murder another, and the alleged incitement is by letter, evidence of the receipt of the letter must be given if the charge is to be upheld. Another significant state trial was that the Irish MP-elect known as Colonel Lynch, who was tried for treason when it was discovered, in the course of his election campaign for the seat of Galway City, that he had fought against Britain during the South African War as commander of the Irish Brigade. During this trial, when the law courts were besieged by an enormous crowd of curious sightseers, Carson had on one occasion great diffi- culty in getting past the police and into the building. 'I'm the Solicitor-General,' he told the policeman at the door. 'That's what they all say,' was the reply. Lynch was found guilty and actually condemned to death, the senior judge reading the verdict on the verge of tears. The death sentence was commuted to penal servitude, and after a few months Lynch was released. He was subsequently elected MP for West Clare, which he represented until 1918. He bore Carson no ill-will. 'He had done his part in condemning me to death,' he wrote in his autobiography, 'but these are not the things that induce bad blood among men of understanding.' Eventually Lynch became a colonel in the British army during the 1914—18 war and conducted a recruiting campaign in Ireland![2]

Two months later Carson led for the Crown in one of the most gruesome murder cases of the time. The accused was a publican of Polish birth known as George Chapman, though his real name was Severin Klosowski, and he was charged with murdering a young barmaid who had been living with him as his wife. A post-mortem examination revealed that she had been poisoned, over twenty grains of antimony being found in her body. The police were now led to suspect that he might have poisoned two other women as well. Their bodies were exhumed and found to be in a perfect state of preservation, the peculiar characteristic of antimony poisoning. The discovery was then novel, and Carson explained it to the jury. 'We have wakened these poor women from their long sleep', he said, 'to give unassailable evidence against the prisoner.' As for the motive, Carson established that it was simply 'heartless and cruel lust'. Chapman was found guilty and hanged. It was later discovered that before coming to England he had married a woman in Poland and had then beheaded her. Gruesome as the case was, it had an even more sinister footnote. Chief Inspector Abberline of Scotland Yard was convinced that Chapman was the key to the most famous of all unsolved sadistic murders, those committed by 'Jack the Ripper' in 1888 and 1889. These murders all took place in Whitechapel, where Chapman was then living. The Ripper had medical knowledge, and Chapman had once been a medical student. The murders ceased in 1890, when Chapman went to America and settled in Jersey City. Between 1890 and 1892 similar murders took place in Jersey City and ceased when Chapman returned to England. If he was not the Ripper, the coincidence is very remarkable.[3]

The strain of heavy work in the courts and in parliament told on Carson's constitution, though it was always clearly a good deal stronger than he himself was prepared to believe. His doctor recommended a spell at one of the foreign spas, and Carson went to Homburg, the watering place in the Rhineland which Edward VII had made fashionable. Besides its chalybeate and saline springs, it had a tennis club and a casino, famous long before that of Monte Carlo. Carson liked the company there, and his visit to Homburg became an annual event. This was a new kind of life for Sir Edward and Lady Carson, enjoying the company of leisured society, mixing with the wealthy and famous, and having sufficient money of their own for material comfort and occasional luxuries. Curiously, in view of his professional acuteness, Carson was always rather absent-minded, and overwork made this trait more pronounced. He was careless about money too. On one occasion when he was spending Christmas at the Hotel Metropole in Monte Carlo he lost £250 in banknotes. He had left them in his dressing-room when he went to his bath, and when he came back they were gone. He got another barrister who was staying in the hotel to go post-haste and stop the numbers at the casino, the railway station and the bank. But later in the day he found the roll of banknotes stuffed into the pocket of his pyjamas.[4]

These short holidays and rest-cures were well-deserved breaks in an extremely arduous life. At the end of the parliamentary session of 1903 Carson felt himself to be mentally and physically exhausted. Yet a task more exacting than any previous case was still reserved for him. He was asked, with little more than a month's notice, to appear for the British government in a complicated international dispute with the United States of America over the boundary of Alaska. He recalled afterwards that he 'went home and cried like a child'. It was imperative to find someone who would help him with the gigantic task of mastering the legal detail of this complex question. From time to time legal work was sent out to be 'devilled' by other men at the Bar, and he remembered that the notes of one of these 'devils' on an international case had seemed to be the work of a very learned and experienced lawyer. He sent for the man and was astonished to discover that he was a young barrister called John Simon, not long down from Oxford. Simon, for his part, found the Solicitor-General almost in a state of collapse. He was only too willing to take on the work of assisting him in order to find distraction from his personal grief, for he had recently lost his wife after only four years of marriage.

Carson took a house on the Solent, looking across to the Isle of Wight, and there the two lawyers set to work for the next few weeks. Simon, who was one day to be Lord Chancellor, later recalled the kindness of the welcome given him by Lady Carson and the family, and how at weekends he spent happy hours playing cricket with young Walter and his friends or

pottering up the river in a new launch which Carson
had acquired. The arbitration tribunal sat for nine-
teen days in the autumn of 1903 and eventually made
an award favourable to the United States. A potential
cause of friction between two friendly powers was
thus settled by legal arbitration, though it naturally
increased Canadian demands that the dominion should
have its own treaty-making powers.

In 1904 Carson was fifty. Two years earlier the
ageing Salisbury had retired from political life, and
Balfour was now Prime Minister, though there were
increasing signs that the long spell of Conservative
government might be coming to an end. Early in 1905
Carson was offered a judgeship in the High Court as
President of the Probate, Divorce and Admiralty
Division. Balfour may have wanted him to accept it
and withdraw from politics, and it was a tempting
offer, but he ultimately declined it, acting (he claimed)
on instinct. Less than two months later Balfour offered
him the Chief Secretaryship of Ireland in succession
to Wyndham.[5] Although it was not generally known
at the time, Carson actually held the office for a day,
but he asked Balfour to relieve him of it almost at
once, characteristically because he believed on reflec-
tion that it might embarrass his old colleague Atkinson,
who as Irish Attorney-General was subordinate to the
Chief Secretary. There were other complications, for
the appointment was made in the wake of the 'devolution crisis' precipitated by the action of the Under-
Secretary, Sir Antony MacDonnell, in drafting a
scheme, virtually on his own initiative, for transferring
a measure of administrative control from Westminister
to Dublin. The Ulster Unionist MPs were immediately
up in arms, suspecting that this was Home Rule by
stealth, and shortly afterwards the Ulster Unionist
Council was brought into existence, a body with
which Carson was soon to have much to do.

Balfour, after clinging on to office with some deter- mination, at last resigned on 4 December 1905. The King sent for Sir Henry Campbell-Bannerman, the leader of the Liberal Opposition, and asked him to form a government. A general election followed in the next year, and the result was a Liberal landslide, 396 Liberals being returned with 51 Labour and 83 Irish Nationalists against 157 Conservatives and Unionists. It was the worst defeat the Conservatives had ever suffered at the polls; even Balfour lost his seat. Carson, representing Dublin University, was fortunate in having no worries on that score, and having to give up office meant that once again he was free to devote a major part of his energy to his practice.

Carson and Rufus Isaacs were now the outstanding advocates of the day. Their rivalry became a legend, and they appeared on opposite sides in many famous cases. While they shared certain qualities, each for example being devastating in cross-examination, their differences were more striking. Isaacs had a gift for mastering detail, especially figures, which Carson could not emulate, and he was much smoother and more tactful in handling judges and juries. Carson had a less formal manner which was often highly effec- tive. He bantered witnesses in a way which Isaacs could not, sometimes playing the stage Irishman in order to lead them on, or mocking their tone or voice, or flaying them with sarcasm, to get what he wanted from them. A trick which he had learned in one of his very first cases was the direct simple ques- tion, for in Ireland the rehearsal of witnesses for elaborate legal duels with counsel was a skilled art. Unlike Isaacs, he had a flair for the dramatic. He was an actor who first made sure of his case, and then pleaded it so passionately that he convinced both judge and jury.

Isaacs was cool and composed in manner and [64] appearance, his wig and gown invariably neat and in place. Carson's wig, which looked small and shabby — it was a relic of his early days at the Irish Bar — was usually pushed to the back of his head. Isaacs, small and neat, with handsome features and alert eyes, always looked the picture of health. His mood was generally optimistic and cheerful. Carson, with his tall ungainly frame, his pale hatchet face and deep-set eyes, was a prey to hypochondria. 'My dear Rufus,' he would say, 'I don't know how I shall get through the day. I ought to be in bed.' Isaacs was not deceived, though witnesses sometimes were. As soon as the time for action came, Carson forgot all about his aches and pains and showed no signs of illness or fatigue. His temperament did not permit him to coast through a case on half his energy. He went to the limit of his resources, and frequently he was seen to be deathly pale and dripping with perspiration when he ended the examination of a witness or a speech to the jury. The two great advocates were the best of friends, and remained so to the end of their lives. Carson said they only ever had one row, though it lasted a long time. 'For it took place in court about twelve-thirty,' Carson recalled, 'and when I went down to my lunch, there was he already eating his without having ordered anything for me.'[6]

The qualities which they displayed were clearly shown in the famous Archer-Shee case of 1909. This case was important because it involved a matter of principle and justice reminiscent of the Dreyfus affair, though without the political furore of that event. It has been dramatised in Sir Terence Rattigan's play *The Winslow Boy*, which in turn provided the basis for a successful film. In the autumn of 1908 a thirteen-year-old Catholic cadet at the Royal Naval College of Osborne on the Isle of Wight, George

Archer-Shee, was suspected of stealing a five-shilling postal order from another boy and cashing it at the local post office. Although he was not accused, his father was requested to withdraw him from the college. The boy repeatedly declared his innocence, and his family, convinced of his truthfulness, eventually sought a legal opinion from Carson. Carson questioned the boy for three hours and was equally convinced of his honesty. The case against him rested ultimately on two pieces of evidence — the opinion of an expert that the forged signature on the postal order was in Archer-Shee's handwriting, and the identification of him by the local postmistress. Carson thought that there was reasonable doubt that she *might* have been mistaken, and on the strength of his written opinion the boy's father asked the Admiralty for a judicial inquiry; but after some further investigation the Admiralty refused either to alter their decision or to reinstate the boy.

The difficulty was that in law the Crown was immune from normal proceedings. Had Archer-Shee been a grown-up naval officer, he could have demanded a court martial by right. At length Carson decided to proceed in the only possible way against the Crown, by petition of right. This mode of proceeding depended, however, on establishing that a contract had been entered into by the Crown with the subject. When the action came to court the Solicitor-General argued the preliminary point of law that the Crown was immune from legal proceedings and had an absolute right to dismiss anyone who had entered its service. Carson contended that the point should have been decided before the trial, but the judge ruled against him. This was, in Carson's eyes, sheer injustice, and it brought out all his Irish belligerence. 'This is the grossest oppression without remedy that I have known since I have been at the Bar,' he

protested, casting scornful glances at the Crown
counsel, who happened to be Rufus Isaacs, and
starting to altercate with him until the judge inter-
vened. When he accused the Admiralty of 'a gross
outrage' the judge replied sternly: 'I do not think
you should say that. I know nothing of the facts.
I have merely decided the point of law;' whereupon
Carson, true to form, picked up his papers and
angrily stormed out of the court.

He was now completely committed to proving
Archer-Shee's innocence. An appeal was lodged at
once, and the case came on again on 18 July 1910.
This time the judges insisted on finding out the facts.
The Solicitor-General was overruled and the case
came on nine days later before a judge and a special
jury. The young cadet made a good impression in the
witness box as Carson conducted his examination-in-
chief; then he had to stand up to a gruelling two-day
cross-examination by Rufus Isaacs, an ordeal which
he came through splendidly. The key witness was
the postmistress, and in cross-examining her Carson
was faced with a delicate task which demanded the
utmost forensic skill. Employing all his resources of
charm, he had to wipe out the damaging effect of her
examination-in-chief, leading her on gently to create
an impression that she could just possibly have made
a human and understandable error. She was clearly a
totally honest witness, and he dared not antagonise
the jury by trying to exhibit her as untruthful. In this
he was brilliantly successful, and, when she stepped
down, her honesty had not in any way been im-
pugned. In such scenes the art of the advocate is shown
at its most impressive.

And yet, had the onlookers known it, Carson was
almost beside himself with private worries and beset
by all kinds of handicaps. His wife's health had suddenly begun to cause him acute anxiety, and he had

other family troubles presently to be described. In addition, he had since February taken on heavy responsibilities as leader of the Irish Unionists, who consulted him frequently during the case. As if all this were not enough, London was in the grip of a heatwave, and the atmosphere of the court was stifling. At the beginning of the third day he had to tell the judge that he was unwell because of the heat and might have to ask for an adjournment. 'Perhaps, however,' he added engagingly, 'I may get better as the case proceeds.' He managed to stick it out, and the climax came early the next day, when, to everyone's surprise, the Admiralty suddenly gave in and Isaacs told the court he was satisfied that the boy was innocent of the charge brought against him. When Carson rose to speak, tears suddenly gushed into his eyes. 'The complete vindication of his son, George Archer-Shee, was the object of the plaintiff in bringing this action,' he declared. 'That object has been entirely achieved.' In an emotional atmosphere jurors and spectators surged round Carson and his client and overwhelmed them with congratulations. Nevertheless, the Admiralty did not reinstate the boy, nor did the Treasury compensate his father for the immense legal costs. Eventually, after questions were asked in the House of Commons, a tribunal of which Carson and Isaacs were members awarded him £7,120. Some four years later young Archer-Shee joined the army and was commissioned in the South Staffordshire Regiment. He died of wounds in the first Battle of Ypres, and his name is one of those inscribed on the Menin Gate.[7]

3

Annette's health was now beginning to fail, and Carson, intensely worried about her, was also having problems with all of his children except Aileen, who

was now married. Harry, the eldest, had been a severe
[68] disappointment to his father since 1898. He showed
no inclination to follow in his footsteps, was restless
and bored, and got into debt. After rescuing him
more than once, Carson packed him off to Rhodesia
and through the influence of Cecil Rhodes set him up
as a farmer. He enlisted at the outbreak of the South
African War, and served with distinction throughout
the campaign, as he was to do again in the First World
War. He had no lack of courage, resembling his father
in that at least; but afterwards he reverted to his
rootless, extravagant ways and was for Carson a lifelong cause of pain. Walter, the younger son, had gone
into the navy (like Archer-Shee, he had been an
Osborne cadet) and was serving as a midshipman in
HMS *Albemarle,* but when he came home on leave
Carson found he could not communicate with him.
Gladys, now twenty-four, he regarded as the most
intelligent of his offspring, but her health was delicate.
She developed tuberculosis and was sent to a sana-
torium in Switzerland, where she fell in love with an
American ('I do not relish foreign relations,' Carson
warned her), and when the family later met him
Carson reacted very unfavourably. Puzzled, he con-
fided to Lady Londonderry: 'My children are a rum
lot.'

The years between 1906 and 1910 were not happy
ones for Carson in politics either. Though the size
of the Liberals' majority made them independent of
the Irish Parliamentary Party and enabled them, as
Tim Healy said, to 'put Home Rule in cold storage',
the Irish problem remained as menacing as ever. The
repeal of the Crimes Act had resulted in a sharp
increase in violence. Characteristically, Carson thought
that the Liberals should either enforce the law or
declare openly for Home Rule and hold an election
on the issue. In December 1907 he said in a speech at

Macclesfield that two of his own relatives had been shot dead as they left their place of worship on Sunday in the presence of a jeering crowd. 'I speak vehemently as an Irishman to English people, and say that if you are not prepared to goven Ireland according to the ordinary elementary conditions of civilisation that prevail in every country, then go out of Ireland and leave us to govern ourselves.'[8] These were interesting and significant words.

In 1907 Campbell-Bannerman was succeeded as Prime Minister by H. H. Asquith. A cabinet reshuffle followed, in which the Welsh radical lawyer David Lloyd George became Chancellor of the Exchequer, and the young Winston Churchill was made President of the Board of Trade, though to his humiliation he lost his seat in the resulting by-election. (He eventually won a seat at Dundee.) Carson detested Churchill, chiefly because he regarded him as a turncoat to the militant Unionist principles of his father, Lord Randolph Churchill. The younger Churchill was generally rather unpopular for his bumptious self-confidence, but the gift of prophecy was not given to Carson when he told Lady Londonderry: 'I think W. Churchill really degrades public life more than anyone of any position in politics, and I doubt if he will ever mature into the kind of serious and reliable politician the majority of people have confidence in.'

The Liberals' frustration at not being able to get certain measures through parliament turned their attention to the House of Lords, and although Carson described Lloyd George and Churchill as 'a pair of buffoons' for launching their campaign against the Lords, it was to prove of momentous importance both for Carson himself and for Ireland. Lloyd George's 'People's Budget' of 1909 was a declaration of class war, deliberately designed to provoke the Lords into rejecting it, which they promptly did.

There followed a prolonged constitutional crisis
which ended only in 1911 when the House of Lords
backed down before the government's threat that
it would create enough Liberal peers to pack the upper
chamber. By the Parliament Act of 1911 the House
of Lords retained the right to obstruct legislation for
only three successive sessions. This legislation was of
the utmost significance for Ireland. The first Home
Rule Bill of 1886 had been defeated in the Commons.
The second, in 1893, had passed the Commons but
had been defeated in the Lords. The Parliament Act
now meant that if the Liberal government could be
persuaded to bring in a third Home Rule Bill for
Ireland, nothing could stop it passing into law. By
1910 the Liberal majority had been eroded by
by-elections, and the result of the first general election
of that year obliged Asquith to pay attention once
more to the needs of his Irish allies. The patience
of the Irish Parliamentary Party, now led by John
Redmond, was rewarded, and Irish nationalists generally were optimistic that Gladstone's great design
was at last to be accomplished. Unionists, for their
part, were filled with alarm.

In the first of the two general elections held in
1910 Walter Long, the chairman of the Irish Unionist
Parliamentary Party, who had until then represented
South Dublin, was returned for a London constituency. The Unionist MPs were therefore obliged to
seek a new leader just as the Home Rule question
threatened once more to dominate Westminster
politics. Early in February 1910 their honorary secretary, J. B. Lonsdale, carried to Carson in his chambers
the fateful invitation to assume the leadership. He
pondered it carefully. In the circumstances it was no
longer simply a post of party responsibility, for it
implied also assuming the leadership of the very determined resistance which the Ulster Unionists were

planning to offer to any Home Rule legislation. For Carson to take such a step in his fifty-seventh year [71] meant the deliberate sacrifice not only of chances of promotion to the highest legal and political office, but of income, health and time to spend with his family. On the other hand, he had always reiterated, and with obvious sincerity, that the maintenance of the Union was the sole reason for his being in politics. After a few days' careful consideration he accepted the invitation. 'I dedicate myself to your service,' he told the Unionists, 'whatever may happen.'[9]

To the Conservative and Unionist Party as a whole, the Home Rule issue was not entirely unwelcome, for they sadly needed a cause which would unite them after the divisions created by the tariff reform question and the bitter struggle over the House of Lords. Party morale was low because of two successive election defeats, and criticism of Balfour's leadership had become strident. Not all Conservatives were opposed to the idea of self-government for Ireland, however, and this was a cause of great anxiety to Carson. In 1910 Winston Churchill and Lloyd George, irked by the Liberal government's dependence on the Irish Parliamentary Party, had been attracted by the idea of achieving an Irish settlement through a coalition with like-minded Conservatives. They began by confiding in F. E. Smith, the brilliant and witty young Conservative KC, who was fast becoming as formidable an advocate as Carson himself, and through him they approached Balfour. The scheme was to grant devolution to Ireland in some roundabout way, the most promising proposal being the federal ideas of F. S. Oliver. 'How can anyone suppose', Carson wrote to Lady Londonderry, 'that those of us who have fought all our lives to prevent a separate parliament and executive in Ireland can now turn round and allow so base a surrender? We are all drifting and I don't know where to. I hate the whole situation.' At the same time Smith was writing secretly to Austen Chamberlain that Home Rule was 'a dead cause for which neither the country nor the party cares a damn outside Ulster and Liverpool'. Balfour was briefly tempted by the thought of a coalition, but in the end he told Lloyd George that he could not become another Robert Peel in his party.

Carson was deeply distressed by hints of this potential treachery at a time when he was worn out by ill-health and domestic worries. As leader of the Irish Unionists he was under great pressure to stiffen the sinews of the Conservative Party on the Home Rule issue. The Irish question was deliberately avoided by the Liberals in the second general election of 1910, and Unionists were subsequently able to claim that they had no mandate from the people for Home Rule when it became clear that Asquith had decided to go ahead with a Home Rule Bill. It was now imperative for the Unionists to organise a campaign to win over public opinion in order that Asquith might be stopped. Carson naturally turned first to that part of Ireland where support for the Union was strongest, and he consulted the Ulster MPs on tactics. The Orange leader Colonel Saunderson had died in 1906, and their spokesman was now Captain James Craig, the MP for East Down. Craig was a bluff Belfast stockbroker, stolid and imperturbable, with a face which seemed to be hewn from Mourne granite. His mind, however, was alert and shrewd, and as methodical as his neat, clerkly handwriting. Both men knew that resistance to Home Rule must be for the most part outside parliament and that this would require a great deal of organisation. Craig suggested that Carson should at once come to Ulster and open the campaign there. Carson agreed, leaving all the details to Craig, who wrote to his wife: 'He says I may fix up the whole programme, and he will carry it out.'[10]

Carson prepared the ground for the Ulster cam- paign as carefully as he did for any of his cases. 'What I am very anxious about', he wrote to Craig, 'is to satisfy myself that the people over there really mean to resist. I am not for a mere game of bluff, and unless men are prepared to make great sacrifices which they clearly understand, the talk of resistance is of no use.'[11] That there could be no doubt on that score Craig was soon to prove. He organised a monster protest demonstration at his home at Craigavon, on the shores of Belfast Lough. Its aim was both to demonstrate the strength of loyalist feeling and to introduce Carson to his Northern supporters. It took place on Saturday 23 September 1911, and despite rain in the early part of the day it was an enormous success. More than 50,000 men from Orange lodges and Unionist clubs in every part of the province marched from Belfast to Craigavon, where Carson told them:

> I know the responsibility you are putting on me today. In your presence I cheerfully accept it, grave as it is, and I now enter into a compact with you, and every one of you, and with the help of God you and I joined together . . . will yet defeat the most nefarious conspiracy that has ever been hatched against a free people.

He then revealed to them exactly what the implications of such a stand might be:

> We must be prepared . . . the morning Home Rule passes, ourselves to become responsible for the government of the Protestant Province of Ulster.[12]

Reports of the speech caused a sensation on the other side of the Irish Sea. On 3 October at Dundee Churchill said that the government would introduce a Home Rule Bill in the next session 'and press it

forward with all their strength'. He urged his listeners
to ignore the frothings of Carson — they would find
that civil war would evaporate in uncivil words. The
population of the nine-county province was equally
divided between Catholics and Protestants, and Carson
had been 'elected Commander-in-Chief' of only one
half of Ulster. These speeches were the first rumbles
of the approaching storm.

4

Just why Carson, at the age of fifty-eight, having
scaled the greatest heights both in law and in politics
and with perhaps even more prestigious offices almost
within his grasp, should have risked his career and
reputation by putting himself at the head of the
Ulster resistance to Home Rule is not completely
clear. It is true that the Union was, as he declared,
'the guiding star' of his political life, and it was
entirely in character that he should be prepared to
make great sacrifices on a point of principle. All his
experience had been in the South, however, or in
England, and he had very little first-hand knowledge
of the reserved and determined Protestants of Belfast
and the northern rural areas, though he knew much
about their embattled history. Part of the explanation
for his apparently reckless espousal of their plans for
resistance may be found in what was going on behind
the scenes in the Conservative Party in the autumn of
1911. At the end of October Lady Londonderry
dined with Carson in London and discussed with him
the leadership of the party. Balfour must soon retire.
She knew that Walter Long wanted to succeed him,
but that Austen Chamberlain and his Liberal Unionist
friends would do all in their power to stop him. Therefore, in order to avoid a split in the party, she suggested that Carson himself would be a suitable leader,

the more so as the Home Rule issue had revived. The truth was that the aristocratic and more truly con- servative elements of the party were anxious to see a strong man of bold and resolute temper leading the party, which had been divided and weakened by its recent squabbles. 'He did not appear to dislike the prospect,' Lady Londonderry reported, 'but talked much about his health and the Ulster Party.'

It is hardly surprising that a man who had risen to high legal and political office from a humble practice on the Leinster Circuit should be attracted by the leadership of the Conservative Party, with always the possibility of becoming Prime Minister. The key factor was his health. He was going through a bad patch, even for Carson, frequently being confined to bed and urged by his doctor, Mr Bruce-Porter, to try one treatment after another for his neuralgia. He was ill when Balfour resigned on 8 November, though he wrote to him at once: 'What I owe you in my career and life I cannot express.' The next morning Lord Balcarres, the Conservative Chief Whip, told Chamberlain that the Irish Unionists would propose Carson as leader, though 'they did not expect to carry him'. There was, however, another candidate in the field, the Scots-Canadian iron merchant Andrew Bonar Law. J. H. Campbell, who was now the other MP for Dublin University, called on Carson that afternoon to say that Bonar Law would stand down if Carson wanted to put forward his name, but Carson at once declined. To avoid a close-run and divisive ballot both Chamberlain and Long withdrew and agreed to accept Bonar Law as a compromise. There is thus a chance at least that Carson might have taken the leadership if he had wanted it. 'I am of the opinion', wrote Lady Londonderry, 'that, had Sir Edward Carson been properly approached at the beginning of the crisis, he would undoubtedly have led the Party. . . . He

was ill in bed; and we know people of emotional tem-
[76] perament and feeling change their minds, but the idea
being new, he sent a message back to say he would
not stand.'[13]

Bonar Law was as untypical a leader of the Conservative Party as it would have been possible to select.
Though born in New Brunswick, he had spent most of
his life in Glasgow. His father, an Ulster Presbyterian
minister, was born in Coleraine, and his brother was
the local doctor there. For the last five years of his
father's life he visited Ulster every weekend, and he
had the strongest sympathy with the Ulster Unionist
outlook. For Craig and his friends this was an unexpected piece of good fortune; short of Carson
himself, they could not have had a more sympathetic
Leader of the Opposition. As for Carson, he told his
noble correspondent: 'I am in bed again, suffering a
good deal and so weak. I think I am worn out. . . . If
you saw me, you would thank Heaven I was not the
Leader.'[14]

5
'King Carson'

1

Asquith introduced the Government of Ireland Bill (to give it its proper title) in April 1912, but before that the Unionists held another huge demonstration in Belfast, which in effect solemnised the wedding of Protestant Ulster and the Conservative and Unionist Party, represented by Bonar Law and seventy English, Scottish and Welsh MPs. The meeting opened with prayers by the Protestant Primate of All Ireland and the Moderator of the Presbyterian Church, and the singing of psalms. The campaign was taking on the colour of a religious crusade; the emotions at work were not understood, and were indeed derided, outside Ulster itself, and few people in England agreed with George Bernard Shaw, who, while not identifying with the politics of his fellow-Protestants, pointed out that when they sang 'O God, Our Help in Ages Past' they meant business.[1] The next step was to draw up a solemn and binding oath to resist Home Rule which every adult loyalist might take. The original Scottish Covenant of 1557 was suggested as a model, but finally a completely new Ulster Covenant was drafted. Its opening paragraph ran:

> Being convinced in our consciences that Home Rule would be disastrous to the material well-being of Ulster as well as of the whole of Ireland, sub-versive of our civil and religious freedom, destruc-tive of our citizenship and perilous to the unity of

the Empire, we, whose names are underwritten . . .
do hereby pledge ourselves in solemn Covenant
throughout this time of threatened calamity to
stand by one another in defending for ourselves
and our children our cherished position of equal
citizenship in the United Kingdom and in using all
means which may be found necessary to defeat the
present conspiracy to set up a Home Rule Parliament
in Ireland.[2]

Craig planned a series of demonstrations beginning at
Enniskillen (where Carson was met by two squadrons
of mounted volunteers raised by the Fermanagh
gentry and farmers) and moving eastwards towards
the greatest concentration of Protestant population.
On 19 September Carson, bareheaded and smoking a
cigarette, read the text of the Covenant to journalists
assembled at Craigavon. The climax of the campaign
came on Saturday 28 September, 'Ulster Day', when
237,368 men signed the Covenant and 234,046
women signed a similar 'declaration'.

As the philosopher Hobbes observed, 'Covenants
without swords are but words.' It has sometimes been
said that the idea of organising a citizen army was
first suggested by the Craigavon meeting of 1911, but
in fact the idea that Home Rule would have to be
resisted by military means had been put forward in
1886 and again in 1892–93, at the time of the
previous Home Rule scares, and in origin it went back
even further.[3] At their annual meeting in January
1913 the Ulster Unionist Council decided that all
the loyalists who had been secretly drilling should
be united into a single body known as the Ulster
Volunteer Force, limited to 100,000 men who had
signed the Covenant. By the summer its organisation
was well advanced, and it had acquired a commander
in the shape of a retired Indian army general, Sir
George Richardson, who set up his headquarters in

the Old Town Hall in Belfast. More English officers were recruited, the most interesting of whom was Captain Wilfrid Spender. Spender had signed the Covenant and thrown up a brilliant career in the British army because he believed that the independence of Ireland would be a strategic threat to Britain. He organised the transport and communications of the force and drew up plans for the feeding of the civil population in the event of a blockade.[4]

In September the Ulster Unionist Council delegated its powers to an 'Ulster provisional government' which would assume control of the province when the Home Rule Bill was passed. Various departments were set up in the form of committees, and an indemnity fund was launched to provide for casualties and their dependants.[5] If Carson regretted allowing the leadership of the Conservative Party to slip through his fingers, he now seemed determined to make things hot for all and sundry. His illnesses had always a psychosomatic element, and two things usually acted as a tonic for him — the challenge of a difficult case, and the emergence of any threat to the Union. He threw himself into the Ulster campaign with unparalleled energy, despite constant complaints of exhaustion, and regaled the country with the spectacle of one of its foremost legal authorities actually contemplating, in theory at least, a rebellion against the Crown. From the loyalist viewpoint, of course, it was not rebellion against the Crown but against parliament, and Asquith's government in particular, but this did not prevent Carson's enemies (who included three-quarters of his countrymen) from gleefully accusing him of treason and anarchy.

Poor Annette had not the same robust constitution as her husband. She paid her one and only visit to Ulster to be at the Craigavon meeting in 1911. A few months later she suffered a slight stroke, and though she recovered to some extent after Carson returned from signing the Covenant, the improvement did not last. She began to lose ground, and when the Home Rule Bill had its third reading in March 1913 Carson was not in his place in the Commons. He cancelled all his engagements and stayed at Rottingdean, never leaving the house for more than an hour or two at a time. Two nurses were constantly in attendance on Annette. Carson did everything that was humanly possible, but she grew gradually weaker, and for much of the time she was semi-conscious. But shortly before she died she said: 'I want to see my old man,' put up her face to be kissed and put her arm around his neck. The end came on 6 April. They had been married for thirty-four years. Carson was overwhelmed by grief and the inevitable feelings of remorse. 'She was with me all through my career,' he wrote to Lady Londonderry, 'and I did the best I could for her and her happiness.'

Messages of sympathy came to him, including one from the King. The overwrought Carson flung himself into his Ulster crusade with redoubled energy; work was the only antidote to grief.

I am glad to be here tonight [he told the Ulster Volunteer Force in Belfast]. Heaven knows my one affection left me is my love of Ireland. . . . Remember you have no quarrel with individuals. We welcome, aye, and we love, every individual Irishman, even though opposed to us. Our quarrel is with the Government. If they wish to test the legality of anything we are doing, or have done, do not let them take humble men. I am responsible for everything. They know where to find me, for I never ask any man to do what I am not myself ready to do.[6]

And yet the lawyer-politician had always (in the phrase of his ardent supporter Rudyard Kipling) 'two sides to his head'. Since 1912 the Liberal government had been vexed by what became known as the 'Marconi scandal'. Several members of the cabinet fell under suspicion when a sharp rise took place in the value of shares in the Marconi Company just before the Postmaster-General signed a contract with the company to set up a chain of wireless stations throughout the British Empire. Cecil Chesterton, the brother of the author G. K. Chesterton, made a series of libellous attacks on Sir Rufus Isaacs, the Attorney-General, Lloyd George and Herbert Samuel, the Postmaster-General. The Commons set up a committee of inquiry, but at this point the charges were renewed by the French newspaper *Le Matin*. Isaacs and his brother issued writs for libel. Winston Churchill then pursuaded Carson and F. E. Smith to appear for the Liberal ministers. This was a shrewd move, disarming even the most suspicious of the Conservatives. On the other hand, Carson's willingness to act for his political opponents aroused the anger of many of his colleagues and totally puzzled his Ulster followers. Carson's attitude was simply that as a professional advocate he was like a cab-driver plying for hire, and he defended his decision on these grounds in *The Times*. *Le Matin* apologised as soon as the writs were issued and paid the costs.[7]

By the end of 1913 the Ulster Volunteer Force had virtually created a state within a state. It had over 90,000 part-time volunteers, a small full-time holding force, elaborate mobilisation plans, its own communications system, a motor-car and motor-cycle section, and a nursing corps. Carson was photographed reviewing his troops in various parts of Ulster, his Homburg hat at a piratical rake, and grasping in his hand a blackthorn stick. One motive for the elaborate organisation of the volunteers was uppermost in Carson's mind: the need to preserve absolute discipline in the Orange

rank and file, who might easily be provoked into
[82] aggression against the Catholic population, especially
in Belfast and Derry. The UVF directed the agitation
steadily and effectively at the government and, in
Tim Healy's words, provided Carson with a 'safety-
valve for the Orangemen'. Its warlike preparations
were at first regarded as bluff and were greeted with
derision. Many nationalists felt that Carson had
'come a cropper' at last. But the dedication, efficiency
and smartness of the volunteers, their complete devotion to, and trust in, Carson and their unshakable
determination at length began to cause a distinct chill
of uneasiness in the corridors of Westminster.[8]

Militarily speaking, however, the UVF was less
formidable, for it could not really hope to withstand
the British army for long without sufficient arms. The
gospel that only armed resistance to Home Rule would
be effective had been preached since 1886 by a fiery
little ex-artillery man, Major Frederick Crawford.
During 1913 Crawford and his helpers set up a secret
arms network in England and had secretly imported
into Ulster several thousand rifles, six machine-guns
and a large quantity of ammunition; nevertheless, by
the end of the year the rank and file were growing
critical of the leadership because so few weapons
were yet available.[9]

Matters came to a head after 5 December 1913,
when the government by proclamation banned completely the importation of arms and ammunition into
Ireland. At a conference in London the UVF commanders put their complaint to Carson and the other
political leaders, and it was decided that a scheme
should be worked out for the illegal importation of
arms 'on a large scale'. Plans were also made for such
eventualities as the arrest of Carson and the members
of the provisional government. Two days later another
meeting was held, this time at Craigavon, and Sir

George Clark, the chairman of the arms committee of the Ulster Unionist Council, was asked if he was pre- pared to bring in 20,000 rifles and 2 million rounds of ammunition quickly if the emergency arose. Crawford was the only man who could carry through such an operation.[10]

Crawford had earlier outlined to the arms committee a scheme to buy a large quantity of rifles and ammunition in Hamburg, acquire a suitable ship and run the whole cargo into one of the Ulster ports. Some members of the committee regarded him as a dangerous fanatic who might well bring disaster on their cause, and he was kept in check. Now his plan was reconsidered. The risk was enormous, but Craig wholeheartedly supported it, and eventually in January 1914 Carson gave it his blessing, though not without grave misgivings. For him the decision was a much more difficult one. Here was a distinguished King's Counsel, a former Solicitor-General, contemplating an act of breathtaking illegality which might well lead to international complications. Crawford was impulsive and hot-headed; if the plan ended in disaster, the Ulster Unionist cause might just survive, but Carson would not — his enemies would see to that. Two compelling factors influenced his decision: the mounting dissatisfaction of the volunteer rank and file, who were saying openly that the politicians had let them down; and the increasing likelihood of a sudden military move by the government, which, if successful, would bring resistance to an ignominious end. If the UVF were adequately armed, the risk of military action by Asquith would be diminished; and if in the last resort they did have to confront the army, then they must put up such a good fight that their cause might still prevail, even if they were beaten in the field.

The decision once made, Carson left the details to

Craig. The secret was known to only a dozen men,
[84] and it was well kept under trying circumstances for
the next three months. Crawford set out for Hamburg
and arranged to buy from an armaments firm he had
done business with in 1913 some 20,000 rifles and
3 million rounds of ammunition.* To make absolutely
sure, he called on Carson on his way through London.
'Now, Sir Edward,' he warned him, 'you know what
I am about to undertake, and the risks those who
back me up must run. Are you willing to back me to
the finish in this undertaking?' Carson's face was
stern, and there was a glint in his eye. He rose to his
full height, advanced to Crawford's chair and leaned
over it, shaking his clenched fist in his face. Then, in
a steady determined voice, he said: 'Crawford, I'll see
you through this business if I should have to go to
prison for it.' Crawford rose from his chair, held out
his hand and said: 'Sir Edward, that is all I want. I
leave tonight.'[11]

2

In view of everything which has since happened in
Ireland, it is almost impossible to convey the atmosphere of the crisis over the third Home Rule Bill.
British society was split from top to bottom by it,
and the prospect of civil war, not only in Ireland but
in Britain as well, was uncomfortably real. So bitter
were the feelings of the leading actors that London

---

*The number of rifles involved in the gun-running has been exag-
gerated by historians. Press reports estimated the quantity eventually
landed at between 35,000 and 50,000, and these figures were not
denied by the Unionists. The total number landed in April 1914 was
in fact 24,600. Of these 20,000 were German and the rest Italian. The
quantity of ammunition imported has been similarly overestimated.
For a detailed examination of the question see Stewart, *The Ulster
Crisis,* Appendix, 244—6.

hostesses dared not mix them at the dinner table; it became, as one wit said, 'war to the knife and fork'. [85] Leading figures in British public life gave Carson and his cause their unstinted support. Lord Milner put his unrivalled influence and experience at Carson's service, even offering to explore some means to *'paralyse the arm* which might be raised to strike you'[12] (that is, to tamper in some way with the army) and to take Carson's place if he were arrested. Generous financial support came from sources which might now seem surprising: from Waldorf Astor and Lord Rothschild, from Lord Iveagh and the Duke of Bedford, Rudyard Kipling and Sir Edward Elgar.[13]

The question of the army was delicate in the extreme. Could its officers, Conservatives almost to a man, be relied on to take the field against Ulster's loyalists if the worst should come to the worst? Would the Royal Navy blockade Ulster's coast? All this debate was set against the ever-darkening sky of international relations. In Germany Kaiser William II was watching England's Ulster crisis with considerable interest.

In the summer of 1913 the Kaiser had an opportunity of meeting Carson, whose doctor had packed him off to Homburg because he was so run down. The meeting was purely social, but it naturally aroused suspicions that some connection was being formed between Germany and the Ulster Volunteer Force. The Kaiser said wistfully that he would have liked to have visited Ireland, but his grandmother, Queen Victoria, would never let him. 'I think, sir, you are well out of it,' was Carson's reply.[14] All this served, nevertheless, to accentuate the gravity of the political situation, and several initiatives were taken to try to find a political solution which would avert a collision. In the autumn Lord Loreburn, a Liberal ex-Lord Chancellor, wrote to *The Times* pointing out that the

Home Rule Bill would be law by June 1914, and
[86] urging the ministers 'who assuredly have not taken
leave of their senses . . . to consider proposals for an
accommodation'. He suggested a conference in order
to effect a settlement by consent. Carson welcomed
the suggestion, though it obviously alarmed Redmond.
Bonar Law went to Scotland to see King George V
and assured Churchill, the minister in attendance at
Balmoral, that Carson would undoubtedly set up his
provisional government when the time came.

Afterwards he wrote to Carson: 'As you know, I
have long thought that if it were possible to leave
Ulster as she is, and have some form of Home Rule
for the rest of Ireland, that is on the whole the only
way out.' Carson's reply was distinctly more moderate
than his public attitude:

> As regards the position here I am of opinion that
> on the whole things are shaping towards a desire to
> settle on the terms of leaving 'Ulster' out. A diffi-
> culty arises as to defining Ulster. My own view
> is that the whole of Ulster should be excluded but
> the minimum would be the six plantation counties,*
> and for that a good case could be made.[15]

Churchill had always privately declared himself in
favour of some kind of special treatment for Ulster,
and from this point it was possible to discuss openly
the possibility of partition. The talks which followed
achieved nothing, for Asquith could not go back on
his pledges to Redmond, and Redmond could never
accept any proposal which would divide Ireland. By
the spring of 1914, however, partition in some form

---

*Carson's history was here at fault. He meant the six counties with
large Protestant populations which now constitute Northern Ireland,
not the six counties of James I's Ulster plantation, which did not
include Antrim and Down.

had become established as the only basis for discussion of a settlement. On 9 March 1914 Asquith put his last proposals for a compromise before the Commons, a scheme to give each of the Ulster counties the separate option of staying out of Home Rule for six years, after which time they would be automatically included, unless parliament decided otherwise in the interval. Carson at once rejected the offer as a 'sentence of death with a stay of execution for six years', though Redmond consented to it as a last resort. For two whole years Asquith had procrastinated on Ulster, hoping that some turn of circumstance would provide a way out. Now, using the pretext of a breakdown in the talks, he reluctantly gave his consent to a plan masterminded by Churchill, the First Lord of the Admiralty, and Seely, the Secretary of State for War, to overwhelm the Ulster Volunteers by a swift and decisive military action. Two battalions of infantry were to be moved to Ulster, and the garrisons of Enniskillen, Omagh, Armagh and Newry, surrounding the main area of UVF activity, were to be reinforced. Troops landed by destroyer were to secure Carrickfergus and Holywood on either side of Belfast Lough. A squadron of warships was to be assembled at Lamlash in the Firth of Clyde, and the navy had been ordered to support the army 'with guns and searchlights'. General Macready, who was notoriously hostile to the Ulster Unionist movement, was appointed military governor of Belfast in all but name. The operation was to take place at daybreak on 21 March.

Carson got wind of what was planned at the War Office, almost certainly from Sir Henry Wilson, the Director of Military Operations, who was a warm supporter of the Ulster Unionist cause. According to one account, he also learned from an Ulsterwoman who was the wife of a high official that he and Craig

were to be arrested. Both men knew what the con-
[88] sequences of this would be in Ulster, and therefore
decided to go there without delay. Craig left London
on Wednesday 18 March, Carson waiting until the
next day to take part in the censure debate in the
House of Commons. In his best fighting form he
raked the front bench, describing them as a 'government of cowards' who were going to 'entrench themselves behind His Majesty's troops', and then, after a
short and very unparliamentary exchange with Joseph
Devlin, the Nationalist MP for West Belfast, he
stalked out of the House in characteristic fashion,
pausing by the Speaker's chair to acknowledge the
Opposition cheers and declare: 'I am off to Belfast.'
At 5.55 p.m. he boarded the boat train at Euston,
telling an eager *Daily Express* reporter: 'I go to
my people.'

Craig had meanwhile transferred the entire headquarters staff of the UVF from the Old Town Hall in
Belfast to his residence at Craigavon. Units of the
force were mobilised and put on stand-by, and the
'Special Service Section', along with the motor-cycle
corps, met Carson next morning on his arrival at the
Belfast docks. Their commander, Captain Crozier,
later wrote that his orders were clear and definite.
If Carson had been arrested, he was to 'wipe out' the
police;* but fortunately as Carson came down the
gangway Crozier received a broad wink from 'a burly
police sergeant from Derry', and so was not required
to set the match to civil war. Carson was whirled

---

*Instructions concerning the arrest of the RIC were issued by
Carson on 18 March and are recorded in a letter written on 21 March
by General Sir William Adair commanding the Antrim Division (O'Neill
Papers, D1238). On mobilisation the police were to be arrested and
disarmed, but under no circumstances were the volunteers to use
firearms until they were fired on.

away by car to Craigavon, accompanied by the motor-cycle escort. There Crozier's West Belfast volunteers took over the guard duties, and the house went into a state of siege.[16] Captain Spender's wife described the scene in her diary:

> There was a tent by each gate, with a number of men on guard, in plain clothes except for puttees, bandoliers, and military greatcoats; in a field by the house was a large tent with a small hospital tent beside it. On the lawn there were batteries of press cameras waiting to pounce on Sir Edward as soon as he should appear. We went in to tea with Captain and Mrs Craig. . . . Sir Edward came in. . . . We talked a little, but he was coughing and looked tired so I wouldn't bother him.[17]

To this embattled mansion UVF dispatch riders brought astounding news on Friday evening of the resignation of 'practically all the officers of the cavalry regiments' stationed at the Curragh, Co. Kildare. What had happened was that Sir Arthur Paget, the GOC in Ireland, had explained his orders so confusedly to his senior staff that fifty-seven cavalry officers, led by their brigadier, Hubert Gough, had declared that they would prefer to resign if ordered north. At seven o'clock that evening Paget telegraphed the War Office: 'Fear men will refuse to move.' Next day screaming headlines in the papers announced a 'mutiny' at the Curragh. The Ulster crisis had become the army crisis.

Belfast, unconscious of the fate intended for it, awoke on Saturday morning and puzzled over the two strange warships which had appeared in Belfast Lough. For various interacting reasons, of which the Curragh affair was only one, the entire operation had been bungled. Letters and telegrams poured into Craigavon from all over the world. By a safe messenger

Carson sent a letter to his daughter Aileen:

> We are all peaceful here and it is the Government
> who have the jumps. Of course if the Government
> had attempted to interfere with us it would have
> been the beginning of the end. They seem to have
> climbed down and made a mess of everything and
> now they are begging the men to come back. . . .
> Have no anxiety — all will be well somehow and in
> any event we are all prepared to suffer and of that
> you may be proud.[18]

3

While these dramatic events were taking place in
Ireland, Crawford was perfecting his plans in Hamburg.
His rifles were loaded into lighters, taken through the
Kiel Canal into the Baltic, and there transferred to
the Norwegian steamer *Fanny* which he had previously
purchased in Bergen. Totally unaware of the crisis, he
escaped into the mists of the Baltic and crossed the
North Sea. But he had been obliged to give the slip to
Danish customs officials who had ordered the ship to
heave to, and next day English newspapers carried the
startling but inaccurate headline 'ULSTER'S MYSTERY
ARMS-SHIP CAPTURED'. At Craigavon this news had a
shattering effect, for over £70,000 had been invested
in the plan. 'Now we must begin all over again like a
general after a defeat,' said Carson as he sat down at
the dinner table. 'We must have a new plan.' On this
scene there suddenly burst like an accusing spectre
the angry Crawford, who had come ashore at Tenby
and taken the Irish Mail to Belfast. Craig stretched
out his hand to him, and then, as Crawford later
wrote, 'I did a cruel thing: I swept his hand aside and
regretted it the same moment. I said "I will shake
hands with no member of the Committee until I
know what they propose to do with the *Fanny*'s

cargo.'" Craig, unruffled, put his arm round Crawford's shoulder and said: 'It's all right, Fred, the Chief is here.' And Carson, recognising a kindred spirit, took Crawford's part. The guns would not be taken back (Crawford had threatened to put them ashore on the Ards peninsula) and the final details would be left to him.[19]

A vital decision had now to be made on the exact location for the landing of the arms. Craig and Crawford were strongly in favour of 'a big military operation' at Belfast, unloading the rifles under cover of large-scale manoeuvres by the UVF, but Colonel Frank Hall and some of the others who were in the secret thought it safer to choose the small port of Larne in Co. Antrim. Crawford had vowed at Craigavon that he would accept no change in his instructions without Carson's signature, so Hall crossed to London to see Carson. He found him in bed and looking 'distinctly worried', but after discussion Carson agreed to the alternative plan. The mobilisation of the volunteers at Belfast was allowed to proceed, however, and provided an excellent diversion which effectively deceived the authorities.[20]

Near the Tuskar light the rifles were transferred in open water to a much less conspicuous coal-boat, the s.s. *Clydevalley,* and during the night of 24—25 April they were landed at Larne, Donaghadee and Bangor, ports on the east coast of Ulster, and secretly distributed throughout the province. A telegram with the single codeword 'Lion' brought the news to Carson's London home.

The Larne gun-running enabled Asquith to regain some of the moral advantage lost in March, but the arming of the Ulster Volunteer Force, coming so soon after the disastrous attempt at coercion, made a return to a strong policy impossible. The question must be settled by negotiation if it were to be settled at all. Nevertheless Asquith's 'wait and see' tactics [92] had not been entirely in vain. Carson's mood in the summer of 1914 became noticeably more sombre and reflective. Throughout the rest of Ireland the Irish Volunteers had been raised in imitation of the Ulster Volunteers, but for the opposite purpose, and they had every intention of arming themselves in the same way. Carson had gambled on Asquith backing down and abandoning the bill altogether, thus preserving the Union and avoiding the need for actual confrontation. Now it was beginning to look as if he had lost. The cards were about to be played. Craig and the Ulster Unionists took a different view. They were absolutely in earnest, and there was no length to which they were not prepared to go to defend their position. If the Union should founder, they even saw some advantage in partition. They could perhaps save themselves. Carson, as a Southerner, could not afford to take that line. Quite apart from the fate of the Southern Unionists as a whole, there was the difficult question of those Unionists in Donegal, Monaghan and Cavan who had signed the Covenant as Ulstermen and supported the UVF to the hilt. How were they to be saved?

Asquith's final attempt to bring Redmond and Carson to a settlement was at the conference held by the King's invitation at Buckingham Palace in July. For a few days the delegates, in Churchill's words, 'toiled around the muddy byways of Fermanagh and Tyrone' in a vain effort to agree about areas to be excluded. A few days later the United Kingdom was at war with Germany, and the potential civil war in Ireland paled into insignificance against the European conflict.

6
Facing the Music

1

On that sunny August bank holiday when the armies of the great powers mobilised, Carson and other members of the Opposition had been the guests of Sir Edward Goulding at Wargrave overlooking the Thames. They were deeply concerned that Asquith would not after all stand by France and Russia. The French ambassador had not attempted to conceal his contempt, and the Russians were convinced that Britain would remain neutral. This news was brought from Westminster by two Conservative MPs. Carson had another visitor, Wilfrid Spender, who came at the request of his friends in the Committee of Imperial Defence to get a decision on the future of the Ulster Volunteers. Carson at once stated that they would be willing and ready to give their services for Home Defence, and that many of them would be willing to serve anywhere they were needed.

The Tories issued an ultimatum to the government which strengthened Asquith's hand in dealing with his divided cabinet, and it was Carson's contribution, during that momentous weekend, to convey to the Prime Minister the support of the loyalists in Ulster. Redmond, with great courage and to his ultimate political cost, made a similar declaration on behalf of the Irish Volunteers. Lord Kitchener, who had just become War Secretary, lost no time in seeing Carson and telling him: 'I want the Ulster Volunteers.' Kitchener had a poor view of politicians, and he took

the line that Carson and Redmond were just a pair of
silly schoolboys who ought to have their heads
knocked together. His first remark to Carson was anything but tactful: 'Surely you are not going to hold
out for Tyrone and Fermanagh?' Carson was not impressed and retorted: 'You're a damned clever fellow
telling me what I ought to be doing.' He and Craig
were determined to keep the UVF together as a fighting unit and suggested that the word 'Ulster' should
follow the name of the division, but Kitchener would
not hear of this and nothing was decided at the time.

Because he had so vehemently insisted on the
loyalty of Ulster, Carson was now in a difficult position. If the Ulster Volunteer Force was taken away,
Asquith might bring in the Home Rule Bill as it stood.
In vain he sought an assurance from him that he
would not do so. On 10 August the Prime Minister
declared that his promise to drop all controversial
legislation would not prevent him from advising the
King to sign the Home Rule Bill. Carson was furious
and feared that the Ulstermen would say he had be-
trayed them, but Craig, as always, was calm and
practical. 'However much we curse and damn the
Prime Minister in the House,' he counselled Carson,
'we must all say the same, that we will do our best
under the circumstances for the Army and the country; then come over here and face the music.'[1] The
two leaders again saw Kitchener and offered him,
without conditions, 35,000 of the volunteers, whereupon Kitchener at last agreed to the inclusion of
'Ulster' in the designation of the units which might
be formed. As soon as he left the War Office, Craig
took a taxi to the firm of Moss Brothers and ordered
10,000 complete uniforms.

On 3 September Carson presided at a meeting of
the Ulster Unionist Council in Belfast, at which these
arrangements were approved. 'England's difficulty is

not Ulster's opportunity,' he told the delegates to frantic cheering. 'However we are treated, and how- ever others act, let us act rightly. We do not seek to purchase terms by selling our patriotism.' Asquith adjourned the House of Commons for a fortnight, and when it reassembled he obtained an adjournment of a further ten days. 'The Irish on both sides are giving me a lot of trouble just at a difficult moment,' he confided to his diary. 'I sometimes wish we could submerge the whole lot of them and their island for, say, ten years under the waves of the Atlantic.' Finally, on 15 September, he told the House that the Home Rule Bill would become law on the 18th. Hoping to appease both Irish parties, he declared that it would be accompanied by a bill to suspend its operation for the duration of the war, and that an amending bill would be introduced in the next session to give parliament a full opportunity of 'altering, modifying, or qualifying its provisions'. He also paid tribute to the patriotic spirit of the Ulster Volunteers, which, he said, had made the coercion of Ulster 'unthinkable'. The Unionists were nonetheless infuriated, and Bonar Law retorted that the government had taken advantage of their loyalty only to betray them, yet to squabble over this domestic quarrel in the hour of national danger would be indecent. He then ostentatiously walked out of the chamber, followed by Carson and the entire Opposition.[2]

The Home Rule Bill received the royal assent in the House of Lords on 18 September amid scenes of considerable excitement. As the Commons streamed back to their own chamber someone produced a green Irish flag, emblazoned with a golden harp, and waved it above their heads. Only eight Unionists were present, and Carson was not one of them. On the previous day he had married Miss Ruby Frewen in the village of Charlton Musgrave in Somerset. The wedding was a

very quiet one, having been kept a secret to the last
[96] moment, and only a few very close friends were present. Carson was sixty, his bride an attractive young Englishwoman of not quite thirty. They had first met casually in Homburg in 1912, when Carson saw her watching a game of tennis. He met her again at Homburg in the autumn of 1913, when he was desperately unhappy, and was much attracted to her. They became engaged in 1914. Carson's letters to her on the eve of his wedding would scarcely qualify for a place in an anthology of love-letters: 'Here I am stuck in bed for another day with that horrid pain in my side .... I am becoming a chronic invalid.'³ Nevertheless, his second marriage was a happy one and brought him great domestic contentment for the remainder of his life.

After a few days' honeymoon at Minehead, Carson took his bride to Ulster and introduced her to the Ulster people. He inspected the 1st Brigade of the Ulster Division, for which 21,000 recruits had come forward, 7,500 of them from Belfast alone. Since Sir George Richardson could not continue in command because of his seniority in rank, his place was taken by Major-General C. H. Powell.⁴ The training of the division began under canvas, and then in hutted camps at Clandeboye, Ballykinlar and Newtownards, as well as at Finner on the coast of Donegal. The men were impatient to get to France, but the division was kept for a long time in Ireland. It was not until July 1915 that they were moved to Seaford in Sussex, and October before they crossed the English Channel and made their way towards the calvary which history had reserved for them under the name of the Battle of the Somme.

2

It was a novel experience for Asquith and his cabinet

to find themselves, in the early months of the war, at the head of a united nation, with nothing to fear from parliament or the country. But Conservative criticism of the conduct of the war surfaced again early in 1915 as a result of Churchill's disastrous Dardenelles adventure. When Lord Fisher resigned from the Admiralty in protest at the continued drain of naval reinforcements, Bonar Law gave Asquith an ultimatum. Either the government must be reconstructed on a broader base, or the Opposition would force a debate which might bring it down. Asquith capitulated, and endured 'the most hellish fortnight' of his life while the first coalition government was chosen. Carson entered the government, with unfeigned reluctance, as Attorney-General. Asquith wanted Redmond in too, but this offer Redmond dared not accept, the more so as his popularity in Ireland was already being undermined. Nevertheless, it was galling for him to see the 'uncrowned king of Ulster' thus rewarded for his rebellion. The unforgiving Birrell, the Irish Chief Secretary, told Redmond: 'You cannot imagine how I loathe the idea of sitting cheek by jowl with those fellows.' At the same time the new Conservative Minister of Health, Walter Long, was telling *his* friends how he loathed the idea 'of our good fellows sitting with those double-dyed traitors'.

Lady Londonderry thought Carson ought to have been Lord Chancellor, while another aristocratic admirer, the Duchess of Abercorn, marvelled: 'Was it only a year ago that you were nearly arrested for treason?' Carson gave up all sources of profit beyond his salary and settled down grimly to the very onerous work of his office and of the government in a time of great anxiety and uncertainty. He would have preferred to devote himself entirely to what he knew about, the work of his department, but as a member of the cabinet he was drawn into many unfamiliar

issues. On the whole Carson's conception of the con-
[98] duct of the war agreed with Wilson's and Kitchener's,
that it was going to be a long haul and that optimistic
visions of a speedy victory were mere illusions. It
could not be won by tricks or diversions like the expedition under General Sir Ian Hamilton to Gallipoli,
but must be fought to a finish in the mud of Flanders.
Wilson, who was enthusiastically sympathetic to the
French, seized the opportunity of the entry of his
friends into the cabinet to promote the demands of
the western front and urge the winding up of the
Gallipoli campaign. A cabinet committee had been set
up to deal with the Dardenelles, and Carson became a
member of it after the calamitous landings at Suvla
Bay in the summer of 1915. He had opposed the expedition strongly before joining the government; his
view now was that either it should receive the fullest
support the Allies could give to it (for failure was
bound to damage British prestige in the East) or, if
that were not feasible, then there should be a total
evacuation of the Gallipoli peninsula. As the details
of the fearful losses inflicted by the Turks were borne
in on him he became more and more an advocate for
evacuation. To Carson it was a matter of plain common sense — among the letters that came in to him
were some from one of the divisional commanders,
General Mahon, who had been his schoolfellow at
Portarlington — and as time went on he became so
horrified by the casualties that he began to think of
resigning.

He brooded, too, over the situation in the Balkans,
which had become menacing. Austria was massing
troops on the Danube, and Carson was convinced that
an Austro-German invasion of Serbia was imminent.
On 25 September Bulgaria declared war on the Allies,
and on 7 October the Germans, Austrians and Bulgar-
ians invaded Serbia. When the cabinet met two days

later Lloyd George asked Kitchener if he had heard anything. Kitchener replied that up to the time of the cabinet meeting he had no news from Serbia. Lloyd George thought that news might have come in since, and asked the Prime Minister's secretary to telephone the War Office. The secretary was told that a telegram had come in the previous day, reporting that the Germans had one battalion across the Danube and that the Austrians had crossed the Slava at five places. The War Secretary did not express any great surprise that he had not so far seen this telegram.

When he heard the text of the telegram Carson picked up a piece of writing paper and passed it to Lloyd George. On it he had scribbled: 'K. does not read the telegrams and we don't see them — it is intolerable. E. C.' Carson disliked Kitchener ('that great stuffed oaf'[5] he was heard muttering), and he now went for him as if he were a hostile witness in court, mercilessly cross-examining him with regard to 'places, times, ships and everything else'. The meeting took place on a Saturday, and afterwards Kitchener took Carson with him over to the War Office. When he entered his room he pointed to a box in the corner. 'There you will find Johnny Hamilton's dispatches, which you so much want to see,' he said gloomily. 'You can spend the weekend over them, and damned unpleasant reading you will find them.' On Monday there was a full meeting of the Dardenelles Committee. Carson, Bonar Law and Lloyd George all favoured landing troops at Salonika and going to the aid of the Serbs. The Chief of Staff, Sir William Robertson, then had to reveal that the Salonika railway was not equipped to transport them, even though the cabinet had instructed Kitchener to double the line and increase the rolling stock in January 1915. Nothing had been done. Other ministers pressed for sending reinforcements to Gallipoli instead. So a compromise was

reached, whereby troops were to be sent to Egypt
[100] with a general who would make up his mind where
they were most needed.

That was the last straw for Carson. Serbia was
being left to her fate, and he could not stomach that.
He resigned from the government the next day.
Asquith wrote to him: 'I part from you in hearty
sorrow and with real friendship,' but in truth he was
not completely sorry to be rid of such an embarrassing
colleague. The news that Carson had resigned sent a
shock round the whole country.[6] There had been a
strong feeling that the courage and resolution he had
shown in Ulster might be exploited by the war cabinet,
and people everywhere concluded that something was
seriously amiss at the highest level of decision — as indeed it was. But some of Carson's colleagues criticised
his action as essentially selfish and self-indulgent at
such a critical moment; by staying in the cabinet he
could have strengthened Bonar Law's fight for the
evacuation of Gallipoli. On the other hand, both Bonar
Law and Lloyd George might have resigned with him,
and so brought about the shake-up which Lloyd
George was to engineer a year later. Wilson recorded
in his diary: 'Absolute indecision and chaos reign in
the cabinet, all due to Asquith who has now gone to
bed to gain some more time.'[7]

The evacuation of Gallipoli was at last carried out
at the end of the year, after thousands of lives had
needlessly been lost. Carson now became preoccupied
with the dilatory conduct of the war and the need to
'improve the machine'. A committee of Conservative
backbenchers was formed to forward this objective,
with Carson as its chairman. It was soon co-operating
with like-minded Liberals, and together they were to
exert a decisive influence on the coalition government.
In the meantime Carson had again resumed his Bar
practice and soon appeared in a sensational case in

the Court of Appeal. It was known as the Slingsby case and it concerned the legitimacy of the alleged [101] heir to an old family estate in Yorkshire. The case lasted for sixteen days, and in the course of it Carson was suddenly taken ill and his place in court had to be taken by one of his junior counsel.

His doctor diagnosed a 'tired heart' and ordered him to take a month's complete rest by the sea. A daughter of Carson's old friend Charles Gill had a house at Birchington in the Isle of Thanet, and there in the eventful spring of 1916 he was nursed back to health by his wife.[8] The Radicals in the House of Commons put about the story that he had had a stroke, and even Balfour was disconsolate. 'He's done for, broken down completely,' he told the editor of the *Morning Post.* Carson was annoyed, but he promised his wife to stay in bed until he was completely recovered: '*Then* I'll show them if I'm done for,' he vowed grimly. The state of his health was of absorbing interest, for it was increasingly coming to be believed that he could be the next Leader of the Opposition, and even a possible Prime Minister. Mrs Spender, who was just then helping Lady Carson to organise gift parcels for the Ulster Division, wrote to her husband at the front:

I think he is beginning to realise that he really is needed, and once he grasps that *fully*, I think his body will obey his mind, and all will be well. But he must give up the Law, and that is a terrible wrench, as he hates Politics and loves Law. He hasn't a spark of political ambition, and is incurably modest, astonishingly so.

On Saturday he had a long letter from the *Morning Post* editor, imploring him to give up Law and devote himself to the nation, and emphasising our need of him as a Leader; and on Sunday Mr Gill had a long talk with him on the same subject. But he *is* nervous about his health, and his heart bothers him still, which he thinks more serious than it is.[9]

By the end of March Carson had recovered and was back in his old place in the Commons. The Unionist and Liberal war committees were pressing conscription on Asquith, who, as usual, played for time. Bonar Law was now under Asquith's influence and as a result was estranged from Carson for a time. The conscription issue forced a crisis in April. Lloyd George threatened resignation, and Asquith agreed to a modified form of conscription, but this was not good enough for Carson and his friends, and in the end they forced the government to agree to introduce a measure of universal conscription. The crisis drew Carson and Lloyd George closer together. 'Carson is improving daily,' the latter noted. 'He is a fine fellow.' Despite these civilities, neither man ever overcame the deep distrust which he harboured for the other.[10]

3

The outbreak of the Easter Rising in Dublin on 24 April came as a bolt out of the blue, reviving the whole question of Ireland just when most people in Britain had managed to forget it. Carson at once offered the services of such of the Ulster Volunteers who were not in the army, for the purpose of keeping order. They mounted a guard on buildings in Newry and other parts of Ulster, but they were not needed, as the North remained quiet. One curious result for Carson personally was that he was deluged with threatening letters because he was considered to have given the lead in rebellion with the Ulster Volunteers. One man tried to force his way into his house, and the butler had a struggle with him in the hall. 'Probably he is crazy,' reported Mrs Spender, 'but I've no doubt there are plenty who would like to murder him.'[11]

The Easter Rising had a profound effect on the United States, and it was imperative to placate American opinion at almost any cost and, if possible, persuade President Wilson to bring his country into the war on the Allied side. So Asquith asked Lloyd George to try again for an Irish settlement. What the latter now proposed was that the Home Rule Act should come into operation at once, but that Ulster should be excluded from it for the duration of the war. Carson made it clear in a memorandum, to which Lloyd George agreed, that 'The six counties are to be excluded from the Government of Ireland Act and are not to be included unless at some future time the Imperial Parliament passes an Act for that purpose.'

Carson considered this a considerable concession, and in June he met the Ulster Unionist Council and advised the delegates to accept the 'clean cut' for the six north-eastern counties. He pointed out that the Home Rule Act was now law, and that the six counties' only hope of escaping it lay in the amending bill which Asquith intended to introduce. The council agreed with great reluctance, since it meant abandoning three of the Ulster counties. However, the settlement was wrecked by some of the English Unionists, whom Carson had not consulted before going to Belfast. Both Carson and Redmond were disappointed, and Carson dreaded the thought of fighting all over again for the exclusion of Ulster.

While Carson was addressing the Ulster Unionist Council in Belfast on 6 June he was handed a telegram which was to have momentous consequences. It bore the news that Kitchener and all his staff had been drowned when the HMS *Hampshire* struck a mine off the Orkneys. Asquith took over as War Secretary, but at the same time Lloyd George threatened to resign as Minister of Munitions. He had, he told Asquith, for a long time been profoundly dissatisfied with the progress and conduct of the war, and had it [104] not been for the vital nature of his work he would long since 'have joined Carson'. Bonar Law begged him not to resign, and promised to back his claim to the War Office. Asquith then offered the post to Bonar Law, but too late; he was pledged to Lloyd George. The Prime Minister had thus no choice but to make Lloyd George War Secretary, though he was well aware that in so doing he was arranging his own downfall. 'We are out,' wrote Mrs Asquith in her diary. 'It is only a question of time when we shall have to leave Downing Street.'

Carson continued to harass the government and was drawn ever closer to Lloyd George, who described him as 'a man of resolution, good judgment and inspiring personality' and said privately that he would be quite prepared to serve under him. Carson's estrangement from Bonar Law began soon after his resignation in the autumn of 1915. Bonar Law was reproachful, and somewhat jealous of Lloyd George's influence over Carson. The clash between the two men came in the House of Commons on 8 November 1916 and ushered in the crisis which led to the fall of the coalition. The Carsonites had initiated a debate on the sale of certain enemy properties in Nigeria; it was cleverly engineered to attract the maximum number of Conservatives and Unionists into the division lobby against the government. Carson accused Bonar Law (who was Colonial Secretary) of 'misrepresenting the facts' and 'playing the enemy's game'. Bonar Law replied that the issue was one of confidence in the government and that he was sorry to be at variance with his 'right honourable friend opposite', who he thought was being 'not very polite'. When the division bells rang, only 73 out of a total of 286 Conservatives and Unionists went into the government lobby. The government won by a majority of 114, but largely through Liberal, Labour and Irish Nationalist votes.

Bonar Law's friend Sir Max Aitken (later Lord Beaverbrook) saw the true significance of the vote. Bonar Law was being isolated, and the government would eventually be defeated. Lloyd George sent for Aitken and told him that the war was not being waged effectively, and Aitken agreed to work with him, provided that he did not have to sacrifice his loyalty to Bonar Law. Lloyd George then said that 'Carson would smash Bonar Law immediately, and that the best way out was for the two men to join hands', adding frankly that Carson was helping him to bring in a War Council with plenary powers. At this point Carson himself arrived, and Aitken left.[12] During the next three weeks the 'triumvirate' of Lloyd George, Carson and Bonar Law continued their intrigues. On 24 November Bonar Law was persuaded to support the idea of a War Council of four, with Asquith as president, Lloyd George as chairman with real power, and Carson and himself as the other two. Out of loyalty to the Prime Minister Bonar Law at once revealed the scheme to him, and Asquith vetoed it, demurring at the inclusion of Carson in an inner cabinet over the heads of senior ministers like Balfour, Lord Curzon and McKenna. It would be seen as the price of shutting the mouth of the government's most formidable critic.

Carson and Lloyd George did not care who had the title of head of government, provided that Asquith did not run the War Council. Everything now depended on talking Bonar Law over to this view. At first he was adamant that Asquith must not be relegated to the position of a mere spectator, the more so as his senior Conservative colleagues were opposed to what they saw as the 'further aggrandisement' of Lloyd George. Carson wrote to him on 4 December: 'The only solution I can see is for the P.M. to resign

and for L. G. to form a Government — a very small
one. If the House won't support it, he should go to
the country and we would know where we are.' On
the next day Asquith wrote to Lloyd George to reiter-
ate his resolve to remain in control of war policy. It
was a confused situation, but the essence of it was
well described by Lord Milner:

> L. G. is really making a gigantic effort to get rid of
> H. H. A., bring Carson back and form a real War
> Government. All the perfectly useless members of
> the Government — some 16 or perhaps 18 out of
> 23 — are clinging round H. H. A.'s knees and be-
> seeching him not to give in. No thought of what is
> happening to the country — you may observe. It is
> just their positions.

Later in the day Asquith wrote a second letter to
Lloyd George. He had decided to reject Lloyd George's
scheme altogether, since 'it would not be possible for
such a Committee to be made workable and effective
without the Prime Minister as its chairman'. This
move was fatal, and it led immediately to his downfall. Lloyd George at once resigned. Bonar Law and
the Conservative ministers prepared to do likewise,
and the coalition collapsed. Even before they acted,
however, Asquith had tendered his resignation to the
King. That evening the King sent for Bonar Law and
asked him to form a government. Bonar Law thought
that if he failed, Balfour should be asked next, but
both said that they could head no administration in
which Asquith was not included, and Asquith refused
to serve under either. Lloyd George had no such
scruples, and eventually Bonar Law advised the King
to send for 'the man whose leadership was most likely
to win the war'. On the morning of 7 December Carson
was standing with Lloyd George at the window of his
room in the War Office. An immense crowd had filled

Whitehall, anxious to catch a glimpse of the new premier. Presently the summons arrived from Bucking- ham Palace. 'Go,' said Carson grimly, 'and take what is coming to you.'[13]

4

Lloyd George formed his new ministry with remarkable speed. He at once offered Carson the Lord Chancellorship, but to his surprise Carson declined it. He asserted that he did not want any cares or duties outside the prosecution of the war, but he may also have felt that there might in future arise some difficulty over Ireland which would put him at odds with the government and thus force him to resign. For whatever reason, he had turned down the highest prize in his profession, and this did not altogether please Lady Carson. 'Ruby can't help looking a little rueful over the £10,000 a year and a fat pension,' wrote Mrs Spender to her husband. 'She, very rightly, wants everyone to know he refused the Woolsack.'[14] Lloyd George had planned to create a tight inner war cabinet, and had intended Carson to be a member of it along with Bonar Law, Lord Curzon and the Labour leader, Arthur Henderson. Balfour was to be succeeded at the Admiralty by Carson's friend Lord Milner. At the last moment, however, he decided that Carson should go to the Admiralty and Milner be admitted to the war cabinet. Carson demurred, but Lloyd George assured him that he would always have the right to attend meetings of the war cabinet when naval matters were being discussed. Lloyd George thus explains in his *War Memoirs* his sudden change of mind:

I was convinced that Sir Edward Carson's great gifts would be better employed by giving him a seat in the War Cabinet. I had designated Lord Milner for the Admiralty. In that choice I was overriden by the personal prejudices of the majority of the Conservative leaders against Carson. They all admired but disapproved of him. So Carson was kept out of a place for which he was qualified and fitted to a post for which he was unsuited.[15]

This explanation, according to Lord Beaverbrook, was not the true one for Carson's exclusion from the war cabinet. Lloyd George could have overcome any Tory opposition without difficulty. The real reason was Lloyd George's mistrust of Carson, whom he regarded, with some justification, as a potential enemy. He had been in direct conflict with him over many political issues, not least Ireland, and he habitually spoke of Carson's conduct in derogatory terms.[16]

No one was more aware than Carson himself of the incongruity of his finding himself First Lord of the Admiralty, but he was determined to justify the expectations of him that were appearing in the press. 'This is the man,' declaimed one editorial. 'He gets things done.'[17] He drew up a few simple guidelines and resolutely adhered to them: one was not to become an amateur naval strategist; another was to give the Board of Admiralty and the naval staff a free hand. 'So long as I am at the Admiralty,' he declared, 'the sailors will have full scope. They will not be interfered with by me, and I will allow no one else to interfere with them.' It was ironic that this attitude was ultimately to expose him to exactly the same kind of criticism he had directed so fiercely against the soldiers in 1915, and the irony was deepened by the fact that his chief critic, in private to Lloyd George, was Haig, the commander in France.[18]

Just before Carson took over his new duties Admiral Sir John Jellicoe had been transferred from command of the Grand Fleet to the post of First Sea Lord. Balfour had made the appointment in order to have the best man at the Admiralty to advise on counter-measures to German submarine attacks on Allied shipping. Carson threw himself wholeheartedly into the work, organising the defensive armament of merchant vessels. Early in 1917 the Germans renewed their campaign of unrestricted submarine warfare, sinking all ships, Allied and neutral, on sight, and the tonnage of British shipping sunk began to climb to horrific levels. Every possible idea was tried to counter it. An Anti-Submarine Division was formed, and the greatest scientists in the country worked day and night to develop devices like the hydrophone and the depth-charge. A great many German submarines were in fact destroyed, but there was, as Carson told the House of Commons, 'no single magic remedy'. The most successful counter-moves were defensive rather than satisfyingly offensive — the use of decoy vessels (Q-ships) and, above all, the convoy system.[19]

As the appalling losses inflicted by unrestricted submarine warfare gradually reached the public, the press became very critical of the Admiralty. As early as January 1917 J. L. Garvin, editor of *The Observer,* had written to Carson: 'This submarine business is of course going to be worse. The country is awakening to it. Northcliffe, *Telegraph, Daily News* and all sorts and shades are on to the same track. The thing will spread.' Similar letters came from H. A. Gwynne, editor of the *Morning Post,* and from Northcliffe himself.[20] Lloyd George was an enthusiastic supporter of the convoy system and had convinced himself that Carson was protecting the admirals, many of whom he considered to be opposed to the idea. He began to press Carson to make drastic changes in his department — in fact to 'sack the lot' — and he treated Jellicoe with such studied rudeness that the latter several times asked Carson to accept his resignation, but Carson's irritated response was to back Jellicoe and

the admirals to the hilt. This was not the most prudent
[110] attitude to take, for flexibility was essential if the
challenge was to be met, and intransigence only made
Lloyd George the more determined to have his way.
After a good deal of intrigue with junior officers, in
order to get 'the men with brains' (as he put it), Lloyd
George at last got the backing of the war cabinet for
'peremptory action', and on 30 April he went to the
Admiralty and took command himself, the only time
that a Prime Minister has ever taken such action over
the head of the minister responsible. The Board of
Admiralty was reorganised. A new office was created,
that of 'Controller', and Lloyd George appointed to
it a Scottish businessman, Sir Eric Geddes, who in
1914 had been deputy general manager of the London and North Eastern Railway and had since been
directing railway transport in France.[21]

This was a humiliating experience for Carson, but
Lloyd George had not dared to move him from office
at once. The final blow came in the summer. On 6
July the Carsons had gone for the weekend to the
small bungalow which they now owned at Birchington.
Sometime before midnight they were awakened by a
messenger from Downing Street bearing an urgent
letter from the Prime Minister to say that he wanted
Carson to leave the Admiralty and join the war cabinet,
as originally intended.[22] Would Carson let him know
at once? Carson replied stiffly that he would be glad
to resign, but wanted to think about the war cabinet.
A second letter came next day, full of emollient
phrases. Carson had misunderstood. They did not
want him to leave the Admiralty, but they simply
must have him in the war cabinet. The Prime Minister
would always be willing to have him act as the navy's
spokesman there. It was all Lloyd George's way of
easing Carson out of the Admiralty in order to be
able to put more pressure on the admirals who, in his

opinion, were too rigid, narrow and conservative in their ideas. Carson, as always, could not resist the appeal of patriotism. Nevertheless, as Lloyd George wrote, 'Although membership of the War Directorate was a more exalted and powerful position, I am afraid he felt wounded by the change.'[23]

Carson was indeed very sore. Geddes was made First Lord to the disgust and outrage of the admirals, and Jellicoe was summarily dismissed on Christmas Eve, which occasioned a nasty row into which Carson was reluctantly drawn. Jellicoe and the other Sea Lords understood Geddes to have stated that Carson and Balfour had both agreed to Jellicoe's replacement. Sir Lionel Halsey and three other admirals wrote to Carson to ask him 'if you have at any time in the last three months stated in the presence of others that in your opinion Sir J. Jellicoe was not the best man for First Sea Lord'. They told him that they were considering resignation. Carson indignantly denied the charge and wrote a sharp letter to Geddes, who replied unconvincingly that he had been misreported. Halsey had a satisfactory interview with Carson, and the admirals stayed at their posts.[24]

In his *War Memoirs* Lloyd George strongly attacked Jellicoe for his opposition to the convoy system. When the memoirs were published in 1934 Carson declared this was 'the biggest lie ever told'. He had himself taken Jellicoe to the Prime Minister to explain the situation. Jellicoe was *not* opposed to the convoy system, nor was Carson, but time was needed to organise it. Furthermore, there were not enough escort ships. The entry of the United States into the war in April completely changed that position, making it appear that Lloyd George had been able to introduce the convoy system at once and thus bring about a dramatic improvement in the fight against the U-boat. Historians have generally taken the view that

Lloyd George was right to shake up the Admiralty,
[112] that Carson protected Jellicoe and his colleagues, and
that, though formidable in opposition, he proved to
be a disappointment in office. Like most such verdicts
in history, it is somewhat unjust and over-simple, for
only a part of the story is told. The sensitivities of the
admirals were certainly less important than the loss
of hundreds of lives and the prospect of a humiliating
negotiated peace; and whatever else may be said
about Lloyd George, he knew how to cut red tape;
moreover, it must be said that the convoy at once
proved to be the answer to the U-boat, and by putting
it into operation so resolutely Lloyd George enabled
Great Britain to survive and win the war. But Carson's
Admiralty papers give ample evidence that there was
no lack of will or expertise at the Admiralty, and that
every likely means of overcoming the submarine menace *was* being actively investigated.[25]

Throughout his career Carson had the habit, acquired in court, of hastily jotting down lines of
doggerel about the witness or counsel who was talking. One scrap of paper endorsed in Lady Carson's
hand 'written by Edward at Cabinet meeting on
Lloyd George' gives us his view of the Prime Minister
and his methods:

P.M. [loquitor] :
I curse the *optimistic* views of Haig — I don't
   believe'm
I curse the *pessimistic* views of Jellicoe — relieve him
Let Gough be sacked and Haig be damned
On justice let the door be slammed
Let gossip rule instead of law
I'll rule the services by jaw.[26]

5

As soon as America entered the war in April 1917
strong pressure was brought to bear on Lloyd George,

through the American ambassador, Walter Hines Page, to make yet another attempt to settle the Irish ques- tion. Taking up an idea of Redmond's, Lloyd George now assembled a convention consisting of representatives of the major Irish parties and interests. One hundred delegates, none of them women, attended the opening meeting in Carson's old university. To Carson it looked as if Lloyd George was going back on his promise that Ulster would not be coerced. The fact that the Irish question had again surfaced embarrassed him considerably in the cabinet, and he decided that he would resign in the new year. Since leaving the Admiralty he had been liaison minister for the war cabinet with the Department of Information, whose director was the novelist John Buchan. Buchan was at first delighted with his new minister: 'I have now got a chap who will defend me through thick and thin.' However, his assistant, Stair Gillon, was indignant at Buchan's subordination to 'a battered old war-horse like Carson who knew as much about propaganda as I did about Croce's philosophy', and the author of *The Thirty-Nine Steps* soon became critical and disillusioned as Ireland absorbed more and more of Carson's attention.[27]

The Irish Convention sat in Trinity College from July 1917 until the spring of 1918. It achieved nothing. A vital part in the negotiations was played by the Southern Unionists, who tried hard to prevent the partition of Ireland, since it offered no future for them. It was the last effort of the Anglo-Irish, who were, it should be remembered, Carson's own people. The 1916 Rising had shown them that there was little to be hoped for from the continuation of the British connection as it then stood. In June of the same year the Ulster Unionist Council, equally aware of this, had accepted for the first time the principle of the exclusion of six counties, and this was a further cause

for the Southern Unionists' dismay. The Home Rule
[114] Bill, when all was said and done, was on the statute
book, and it contained no special provisions for the
interests of the minority. The Southern Unionists,
under the leadership of Lord Midleton, therefore
sought to reach some kind of compromise with the
Redmondite nationalists, and in 1917 they produced
their own elaborate scheme for Home Rule. Lloyd
George was intensely grateful to them for this conciliatory approach, and 'the new departure . . . became
an essential element in the government's calculations'
on Ireland.[28] Redmond welcomed it also and told
Lloyd George: 'It rests with you and Carson to make
or mar the Convention. Everyone in Ireland believes
that it is in your power to bring these men to reason,
and if the Convention breaks down I can only repeat
the most serious consequences will ensue immediately.'

From the outset, however, relations between the
Ulster Unionists and the Southern Unionists had been
marked by mistrust and mutual reproach; and when
Lloyd George intimated that if the scheme for Home
Rule found general assent in the Convention, apart
from the Ulster Unionist delegates, he would use his
influence in the cabinet and parliament to make it
law, Carson took this to mean that the Prime Minister
had gone back on his pledge that Ulster should not be
coerced, and refused to make any concessions. In any
event, the accord between Redmond and Midleton
led to each in turn being disowned by his followers.
Redmond eventually withdrew from the Convention.
To one of the Ulster delegates who asked him to put
his cards on the table he replied: 'I have no cards. I
am a leader without a party.'

The Convention failed firstly because of the Ulster
Unionists' refusal to make any concessions, since in
their circumstances they had nothing to lose, and
secondly because of the absence of Sinn Féin, who

boycotted the whole proceedings. It marked the parting of the ways between the Northern and Southern Unionists. The Ulster Unionists henceforth concentrated on saving themselves as the cause of Irish Unionism slowly foundered.

'Ireland is such a worry,' Carson told Lady Londonderry, 'and I am constantly being reminded of my duty, which is apparently to desert my friends and my convictions, which, of course, I will never do.' Later he was to declare: 'The Irish Convention gave me more trouble than almost anything I ever had to do with in relation to Home Rule. In point of fact it eventually drove me out of the Cabinet in the middle of the war.'[29] Carson's action in leaving the government on 22 January 1918 was followed by James Craig, who resigned from the minor post he held as Treasurer of the Household and government whip. Carson immediately went to Belfast, where he was received with all the enthusiasm of pre-war days, and resumed the Ulster Unionist leadership.

After the big German offensive in March 1918, which came dangerously close to success, Lloyd George at last tried to impose conscription in Ireland, something which Carson had always advocated. It was decisively rejected by Irish public opinion. Increasingly the war was seen in the south of Ireland as Britain's war, and no longer a war in defence of gallant little Catholic Belgium. Sinn Féin seized the opportunity to make political capital from the issue and launched a highly effective anti-conscription campaign.

Redmond died in March, disheartened by the failure of the Convention, and with his influence steadily dwindling away. And Carson was now removed from the centre of political action. In May Mrs Spender wrote:

Sir Edward is very depressed and unhappy. He feels it dreadfully being back in Town and yet absolutely out of things. Lloyd George has turned against him completely and is doing his best, very successfully, to turn everyone else in the Government against him too. If Sir Edward writes to him now on any Irish question, he doesn't even answer. Sir Edward is convinced the Government has no intention of bringing in either Home Rule or Conscription, as he has always said from the beginning.[30]

On 12 July he was back again in Belfast to address the Orangemen at their annual celebrations. His speech was revealing about his mood and struck an ominous note for the future. 'Nothing has more disgusted me with the filth of politics than to find men going back on their word to those who have given their lives for the British cause.' Not long afterwards he had to intervene to prevent the Chief Secretary from transferring the rifles of the UVF, kept in stores well known to the police, to the direct custody of the authorities, a move which the Ulster Unionists saw as an attempt to placate nationalist feeling by 'disarming' Ulster.[31]

A few days after the armistice, parliament, which had been elected as long ago as 1910, was dissolved, and a general election was held on a new franchise. Carson had represented Dublin University for twenty-six years, but he had differed with the redoubtable Provost Mahaffy over the Convention; and in view of the fact that Home Rule was now inevitable for the south of Ireland, he now sought a constituency in the North. Under the redistribution of seats the Belfast constitutuencies had been doubled, and it was for one of these new seats, Duncairn, that he was now invited to stand.[32] It was a working-class constituency, far removed from the atmosphere of Trinity, and although Carson's return seemed a foregone conclusion, he conducted a very strenuous election campaign. He was suffering from a bad cold and not sleeping well. 'I imagine it is likely to be my last

election campaign,' he said. Polling took place on 14
December, but the votes were not counted until after [117]
Christmas. The figures were:

Sir Edward Carson (Unionist)   11,637
Major W. H. Davey (Nationalist)   2,449
Dr H. N. MacNabb (Sinn Féin)   249

The Unionist majority was 9,188.

Under the redistribution the Unionists improved
their position, winning 26 seats compared with 18
in the old parliament. Except for three Dublin seats,
however, these were all in the six north-eastern counties. In electoral terms the map of partition was
already drawn. The 1918 election annihilated the
Irish Parliamentary Party, which retained only 6
of the 68 seats it had previously held. Redmond's
successor, John Dillon, was among those defeated.
Sinn Féin candidates swept the polls, but regarding
themselves as representatives of a sovereign republic,
they had no intention of taking their seats at Westminster. Instead they assembed at the Mansion House
in Dublin and convened the first Dáil Éireann. In due
course Carson received his summons as an elected
deputy to this assembly, written in Irish; he pre-
served it as a souvenir.

6

In Britain the coalition swept back to power. Lloyd
George tried to persuade Carson to come back into
the cabinet, but he declined, saying that he preferred
to go back to the Bar. 'I long for a whiff of the Law
Courts,' he told Rufus Isaacs, now Lord Reading.
F. E. Smith became Lord Chancellor and was raised
to the peerage as Lord Birkenhead. Craig was appointed Parliamentary Secretary to the Ministry of
Pensions. Carson's decision to go back to the Bar

swiftly brought rewards, and briefs again began to [118] pour into Dr Johnson's Buildings. At this time he suffered a great loss by the sudden death of his friend and faithful correspondent Lady Londonderry, who had for some time been suffering from heart trouble. (Lord Londonderry had died in 1914.) She was two years younger than Carson, and they had been friends for more than thirty years. He could never forget what he owed to her encouragement and her steadfast belief in the destiny of 'the Solicitor'.

Conditions in the south of Ireland were now very disturbed. Every day came news of outrage and murders, the first drops of the storm that was to be the Anglo-Irish War. The Ulster loyalists, fearful that the Home Rule Act would come into operation without the amending bill promised long ago by Asquith and Lloyd George, looked to Carson for guidance. In Britain the attitude to Ulster had dramatically changed, and the sympathy of pre-war days was giving way to a sense of frustration and a feeling that the Ulstermen had all along thwarted a settlement in Ireland. When Carson told the Orangemen on 12 July 1920 that if there was any attempt to take away their rights as British citizens, he would 'call out the Ulster Volunteers', his speech shocked many people in England, and an attempt was made to censure him in the House of Commons.

In February 1920 Lloyd George introduced the fourth and final Government of Ireland Bill, which repealed Asquith's act of 1914 and attempted to find a way out of the impossible Irish situation by dividing the country into two parts. Each part was to have a parliament of its own, and a Council of Ireland was provided for which might eventually bring them together by agreement. The act was ignored by Dáil Éireann; and the Ulster Unionists, who had no wish for Home Rule in any form, accepted it only as the 'supreme sacrifice'. But to Lloyd George's devious mind it was the first step towards solving the Irish problem in so far as it was a problem for Britain.

The demand of the Ulster Unionists had all along been that Ulster should be retained in full legislative union with the rest of the United Kingdom, and there was a certain irony in the fact that they were now granted a form of Home Rule. They had moreover to accept the 'clean cut' of six counties, leaving the other three in Southern Ireland, and this was a cause of great dissension and genuine emotion in Unionist councils. Some of those who had signed the Ulster Covenant in 1912 had difficulties of conscience over accepting the six-county settlement, and Crawford actually published a pamphlet to explain his position — he had been one of the few who signed the Covenant in their own blood![33] But even in 1912, thanks largely to the Presbyterians, the oath had been interpreted as applying only to 'the present conspiracy' and not automatically binding for the future. In their perplexity the Ulster Unionist Council turned to Carson, as always, for leadership. The business community in the North had accepted the situation more readily than the gentry and landowners, and the majority of Unionists took their view of the matter. Carson believed that they were right, and argued that while taking no responsibility for the bill, they ought not to oppose its progress through parliament. It meant, at the very least, as he cogently pointed out, that they had won the exclusion of the six counties without the fight which he had always dreaded. Ultimately this argument prevailed. Carson took it to be the final solution to the Ulster problem and advised that Unionists should make every effort to work the new administration successfully.

Carson was inevitably asked to become the first Prime Minister of Northern Ireland. He tactfully

declined the honour, saying that the task of opening
[120] a new chapter in Ulster history under new institutions
was one for younger men. Craig was the obvious
choice, and Carson agreed to 'hold the fort' at Westminster. He formally relinquished the leadership of
the Ulster Unionist Council on 4 February 1921, a
few days before his sixty-seventh birthday. He gave
them one final piece of advice:

> From the outset let us see that the Catholic min-
> ority have nothing to fear from Protestant majority.
> Let us take care to win all that is best among those
> who have been opposed to us in the past. While
> maintaining intact our own religion let us give the
> same rights to the religion of our neighbours.[34]

7

In the same month that the Government of Ireland
Bill was introduced in the Commons Carson was sent
his horoscope, drawn up by an astrologer who lived
in Devon. It was accompanied by a long, rambling
letter which earnestly warned him that if he did not
withdraw from the public arena for a while, the stars
indicated that he would meet a violent death. 'You
ought to avoid Parliament if possible, and in any case
keep silent, for I think you will be *shot at*. . . . The
following three or four weeks are the most dangerous
(if you take risks, travel on the Tube, visit Ireland or
Parliament) for the full moon on 4 March might
prove fatal to you.' His correspondent promised, however, that if Carson retired and took up 'astrology and
the hidden secrets of nature', he would 'come to a
peaceful end of existence'.[35] It was hardly in character
for Carson to pay attention to this disturbing prog-
nostication, and, more than most public figures, he
was accustomed to receiving threats and warnings;
but given the situation in Ireland, the threat of assas-

sination was by no means unreal. He had, moreover, an additional reason for anxiety. The letter was dated 15 February 1920, and two days later Lady Carson gave birth to a son, who was named Edward after his father. It was Carson's dearest wish to have another son, and he was naturally overjoyed. Next day, when he entered the House of Commons, he was greeted on all sides with cheers and congratulations which he acknowledged 'with a bashful smile'.

All this time Carson was carrying on with his work at the Bar. His powers seemed to be undimmed in the courtroom, and he was always happier there than in parliament. He had no shortage of work, but he no longer taxed himself to the limit as in earlier years. He showed a friend a brief marked for 4,000 guineas which he was sending back because he had only ten days to prepare the case. 'I could have done it once, but not now!' Early in 1921 he made his last speech in the House of Commons, though no one recognised it as such. A few days later Lloyd George offered him a vacant position in the House of Lords as one of the Lords of Appeal. He accepted the offer and laid aside his barrister's wig and gown at last for the robes of a judge.

7
Betrayal

1

He took his seat in the House of Lords on 24 May
1921 with the style and title of Baron Carson of Duncairn in the County of Antrim. His old partner and
colleague F. E. Smith was on the Woolsack to welcome
him. He could have had a hereditary title for his political services, but he chose instead the life peerage
automatically conferred on a law lord, which meant
that his son Harry would not succeed to the peerage.
In the autumn of 1921 the Carsons bought an old
rambling house called Cleve Court in the Isle of
Thanet. It had twenty acres of land round it, with
spacious lawns and kitchen gardens, and it cost them
only £2,500. 'I hope you will come to Kent,' he wrote
to Bonar Law. 'Our new house is near Minster and five
miles from Margate and the air is splendid.'

When King George V travelled to Belfast in June
1921 to open the first Northern Ireland parliament he
made an appeal to all Irishmen to pause and reach out
the hand of friendship, and Lloyd George used this as
a pretext for one more attempt at conciliation. Revers-
ing all the earlier official attitudes, he opened the
possibility for the first time of negotiating with the
insurgents. The war, initiated in 1919 by IRA attacks
on policemen, was bad from the outset; by 1921 it
had become atrocious. The Royal Irish Constabulary
had been reinforced by the Black and Tans and men
of the Auxiliary Division, who had no compunction
about answering terror with terror. By June 1921 it

was becoming clear that public opinion in Britain would not stand for the continuation of the war on these terms.

So, hoping to profit from the good impression made by the King's speech, Lloyd George wrote to Eamon de Valera as 'the chosen leader of the great majority in Southern Ireland', inviting him to come to talks in London to 'explore to the utmost the possibility of a settlement'. When at length the invitation was accepted and a truce between the IRA and the Crown forces agreed, Carson was, as might be expected, deeply disturbed. Lloyd George told him privately that 'the game is up' and 'we shall have to give in'; he intended therefore to resign. Carson replied that he hoped he would not involve the Conservative members of the government, Austen Chamberlain and Lord Birkenhead, in the discredit of such a surrender. He soon discovered, however, that Lloyd George had no intention of resigning, and, much worse, that the suggestion of talks with Sinn Féin had come from Chamberlain in the first place, with Birkenhead's support. The consequences of this step are too well known to need reiteration. The negotiations between the leading ministers on the British side and Michael Collins, Arthur Griffith, Robert Barton, Eamon Duggan and Charles Gavan Duffy on the Irish, dragged on with apparently little prospect of success until the early hours of 6 December, when the Dáil representatives finally signed the 'Articles of Agreement for a Treaty between Great Britain and Ireland'.

Carson had not spoken in the House of Lords since his elevation to it in May 1921. The implications of the Treaty were shattering for him and for all Unionists who had co-operated with the Conservatives in resisting Home Rule since 1886. They sank deeply into his mind. He saw his life's work in politics thrown away, and he resolved to make the settlement the subject of his maiden speech in the Lords. The debate was on a motion for an address of thanks in reply to the King's Speech, indicating that the Articles of Agreement would soon be submitted to the Lords for approval. Carson had pencilled a few notes on the title-page of his text of the Articles, underlining 'Ireland' twice and noting: 'Ignores Ulster.'[1] He began quietly by remarking that Morley, who had introduced the motion, was a very proper person to pronounce the funeral oration over the Unionist Party. Many years before, Balfour had told Queen Victoria that Carson had 'a bitter tongue'. It was now turned on the government in one of the frankest and bitterest speeches ever made in the House of Lords. 'I speak for a good many,' he exclaimed, his voice vibrating with anger. 'I speak — I can hardly speak — for all those who, relying on British honour and British justice, have in giving their best to the service of the State seen themselves deserted and cast aside without one single line of recollection or recognition in the whole of what you call peace terms for Ireland.'

The government spokesman was Curzon, whose pomposity drew Carson's more seething invective:

One thing the noble Marquess forgot to tell us was how the Government came to the conclusion that these Articles of Treaty were so much for the benefit of the country. . . . There is not a noble lord in this House who believes for a moment that these terms were passed upon their merits. Not at all. They were passed with a revolver pointed at your head. And you know it. You know you passed them because you were beaten. You know you passed them because Sinn Féin with the army in Ireland has beaten you. Why do you not say so? Your Press says so, and you may as well confess it. There may be nothing dishonourable in it.

Having mercilessly dealt with the government's failure, Carson now turned to his colleagues in the [125] Conservative Party. Every word was steeped in the bitterness of defeat:

> At that time I did not know, as I know now, that I was a mere puppet in a political game. I was in earnest. I was not playing with politics. I believed all this. I thought of the last thirty years, during which I was fighting with others whose friendship and comradeship I hope I will lose from tonight, because I do not value any friendship that is not founded upon confidence and trust. I was in earnest. What a fool I was! I was only a puppet, and so was Ulster, and so was Ireland, in the political game that was to get the Conservative Party into power.

His worst reproaches were reserved for Birkenhead, 'Galloper' Smith of the old UVF days, who sat peevishly impassive only a few steps away on the Woolsack. F. E. had signed the Ulster Covenant; he had now signed the Treaty.

> Of all the men in my experience that I think are the most loathsome it is those who will sell their friends for the purpose of conciliating their enemies, and, perhaps, still worse, the men who climb up a ladder into power of which even I may have been part of a humble rung, and then, when they have got into power, kick the ladder away without any concern for the pain, or injury or mischief, or damage they do to those who have helped them to gain power.

It was Chamberlain's turn next:

> The other evening I saw with disgust that Mr Austen Chamberlain ... said he made an appeal to the comradeship of his old friend Sir James Craig to come in and submit to the domination of Sinn

Féin. I could not help thinking that it was very like, after having shot a man in the back, going over to him and patting him on the shoulder, and saying: 'Old man, die as quickly as you can, and do not make any noise.'

He went on to deplore the pressure being put on Ulster to join with the South, and in particular the press campaign:

Why is all this attack made upon Ulster? What has Ulster done? I will tell you. She has stuck too well to you, and you believe because she is loyal you can kick her as you like.

'Loyalty is a strange thing', he said in his conclusion.

I have often – I admit it – when we were threatened because we were loyal in Ulster in times past . . . said to myself: 'Well, why don't you give it up and join the others?' And I never did, because I know I could not, because I know it is something that is born in you, inherited in you, and that it is the safety of the State.[2]

The savagery of Carson's attack shocked and angered those who listened. Curzon writhed and changed colour under it. Birkenhead, nonchalant as ever, told the House that 'as a constructive effort of statecraft it would have been immature upon the lips of an hysterical schoolgirl',[3] but he was, in reality, cut to the quick. When he pointed out that the speech contained not a shred that was constructive, Carson angrily retorted that he had accepted the 1920 settlement in good faith. Although Carson had spoken much about Ulster, the true source of his bitterness, the element which made his speech so reckless and raw, a cry from the heart, was that he was himself a Southern Unionist, forced to realise that England had once more

deserted her most loyal friends. He had quoted Birrell
(of all people) as having said: 'It is a British characteristic, though not an amiable one, that once we are
beaten we go over in a body to a successful enemy,
and too often abandon and cold-shoulder and snub,
both in action and in writing, the suffering few who
adhere to our cause in evil and difficult times.' Until
that night, said Carson, he had never believed it to be
true.

The Ulster Unionists had won a victory of a kind,
though not the one they had hoped for. Carson himself had been defeated. His object had been throughout to save all Ireland for the Union, 'the guiding
star' of his political life. What he faced that day in
the House of Lords was the hopelessness of irredeem-
able defeat and betrayal.[4] To his annoyance it was
only when he had sat down that he recalled Harcourt's
words to him, uttered so many years before: 'The
Conservatives, mark my word, never yet took up a
cause without betraying it in the end.'

At the time few of Carson's contemporaries could
understand the reasons for his action, particularly
those who were politically out of sympathy with him.
Tom Jones, Lloyd George's secretary, recorded that
at dinner on the following day the Prime Minister
asked why Carson was so bitter. He had agreed, if he
did not actually propose, the Boundary Commission
which the Sinn Féin leaders had been offered as an
inducement to sign the Treaty. Jones suggested that
Lady Carson was the explanation. She was young
and ambitious and was dissatisfied that Carson was
reduced to the position of a judge, with nothing more
to say than 'I concur'. Lloyd George agreed and repeated this opinion on other occasions.[5]

Carson now openly proclaimed himself an enemy
of the coalition and was active in trying to re-form 'a
real Conservative Party' from Unionist 'diehards'

whose traditional home was Londonderry House. [128] Curzon and Birkenhead (the latter was annoyed by jests about 'diehards' and 'livehards') now tried to silence Carson by laying down the rule that law lords should not make political speeches. Carson said he was always willing to resign if he did anything that was wrong; he knew well enough that the government was bluffing, but he also took the hint and made no further open attacks on it. He reserved the right to speak about Ireland, though, for the Treaty had turned the attention of terrorists to Northern Ireland, where, in the terrible year of 1922, attacks and outrages, aggravated by outbreaks of sectarian rioting, claimed the lives of 232 people, including two Unionist MPs. In London on 22 May 1922 Carson's friend Field-Marshal Sir Henry Wilson was murdered by the IRA on the steps of his home in Eaton Place, only a few doors from Carson's house. With the onset of the civil war in the south of Ireland, however, and the restoration of peace to the whole island in 1923, Carson's interventions in debates became less frequent. He travelled to Belfast and found conditions there much calmer. He cut the first sod in the construction of a reservoir in the Mourne Mountains to supply water to Belfast, and he received a presentation in the Ulster Hall which brought back memories of the old times. 'Thank you, thank you, thank you,' he said, his eyes filling with tears. 'Never forget me, for I never forget you.'[6]

Early in 1929 his health began noticeably to fail. He was sleeping badly and suffering from recurrent sharp attacks of lumbago, which clinics and spas seemed unable to alleviate. He decided at last that he ought to give up his legal work. He was now seventy-five years old and had been practising law for fifty-two years, and he thought the time had come for a younger man to take his place. He announced his decision publicly on 1 November 1929, and his resignation was accepted with regret by the Labour Prime Minister, [129] Ramsay MacDonald.

2

In the summer of 1928 Arthur Balfour's niece, Blanche Dugdale, was collecting materials for her uncle's biography, and she asked Carson for his recollections. Their conversations, as she recorded them in her notes, provide some revealing insights into Carson's final view of Ireland and the politicians. Surprisingly, when she led him on to the subject of the Treaty and its consequences, he said that in the light of all that had happened he would have preferred a Republic to the Free State. Cosgrave had restored order – he gave him credit for that – but he had done it by executing scores of his friends who held the same opinions as he had done, and 'that was vile'. 'No, I think there'd be more decency in a Republic than in this humbug. In fact I'd rather see a Republic.' He said that he did not object to the settlement so much as 'the filthy way it was done, that midnight meeting, and no provisions for the men who had stuck to us. Surely we could at least have stipulated that we would keep order until they had got going? Was there any reason why we should walk off the battlefield and leave our wounded behind?' Asked if he had not thought it was a losing battle all the time, he replied: 'Losing battle? Never. Why, at the very end when Austen said to me that the thing was inevitable, I said "Rot." Joe would *never* have acquiesced. . . . And to think it was his own degenerate son. . . .' Though no longer on speaking terms with Austen Chamberlain, Carson had met him at a dinner two years before. 'Austen came up to me after the ladies had gone, and he said "Carson, will you shake hands?" I said "Yes – on condition you

don't mention Ireland to me, and because of the
[130] reverence I bore your father." But that's enough
about Austen.' Mrs Dugdale asked: 'Do you hate him
worse than Lloyd George?' 'Austen's a coward,' Carson
replied. 'Lloyd George is a mass of corruption.'

Carson was at length reconciled with Birkenhead
also. One rainy night when Birkenhead was waiting
for his car at the entrance of the House of Lords,
Carson saw him and shouted: 'Jump in, F. E., and
I'll drive you home.' Birkenhead did so. For a moment
they sat in silence and then Birkenhead said: 'You
know, Carson, some of the things you have said hit
me pretty hard.' 'You surprise me,' said Carson. 'Yes,
and perhaps you don't know why they hit me so
hard?' Carson shook his head. 'It was because they
were so damnably true.' Later Carson said with a wry
grin: 'And how could you keep up a quarrel with a
man like that?' With Bonar Law too he was reconciled, and even Churchill was forgiven and sent him
signed copies of his book *The World Crisis*. Winston
and his wife, Clemmie, stayed at Cleve Court in 1924.[7]

3

'I'm afraid old age is not all joy,' wrote Carson on the
eve of his retirement. His preoccupation with his
health was as marked as ever. 'I am sorry to say I still
suffer a lot and can do little or nothing,' he wrote to
an old friend, 'so I just stay here and grouse about my
ailments.' In spite of his happy domestic environment
and his pride in young Ned, now a schoolboy at Eton,
he frequently felt very lonely and depressed. Harry,
his eldest son, and Gladys, his younger daughter, pre-
deceased him. One by one his contemporaries at the
Bar were slipping away. Deprived of those arenas
whose atmosphere was his only stimulus, he was restless and bored. He had never been much interested in

books, other than legal ones, and he passed the time with the latest Edgar Wallace or P. G. Wodehouse. He visited Belfast once more in 1933. The loyalists of Northern Ireland had commissioned the sculptor L. S. Merrifield to cast his statue in bronze, and it was placed on a plinth in front of the new parliament buildings at Stormont. The inscription on the base read: 'By the loyalists of Ulster as an expression of their love and admiration for its subject.' On a rainy July day he saw it unveiled by Lord Craigavon in the presence of more than 40,000 people. When the time came for Carson to speak he had to struggle with emotion. 'I know of no words', he told them, 'to express my gratitude to great people who all through these years never for one moment deceived or deserted me. . . .'[8]

At the beginning of June 1935 he caught bronchial pneumonia, and for a while he was not expected to recover from it. But he fought back, as always, with a lion's courage, and gradually his condition began to improve. In the warm sunny days of the late summer he was able to sit out in his garden, but he was too frail to do much, as he said, except watch the birds. He grew weaker as the autumn advanced, and soon he was confined to his room. The doctors diagnosed leukaemia. (Strangely, the Devon astrologer in 1920 had written: 'I think the state of the blood is poor.') Aileen and Walter were sent for to join Lady Carson and young Ned at his bedside. He died peacefully at 8.35 on the morning of 22 October 1935.

4

In his will Carson left no instructions as to where he was to be buried, but he had told Craigavon that he would like to be laid to rest in Ulster. In a radio broadcast from Belfast later that day Craigavon

announced that Lord Carson would be buried in
[132] St Anne's Cathedral in Belfast and that he would have
a state funeral provided by the government of Northern Ireland. A warship would bring the body to
Belfast. The funeral took place on Saturday 26
October. Shops and factories closed down, and the
shipyards were silent as HMS *Broke* steamed slowly
up Belfast Lough under a leaden sky, her ensign
fluttering at half mast. At eleven o'clock the coffin,
covered by the Union Flag, was carried ashore by two
petty officers and six seamen and placed on a gun-
carriage. In almost complete silence it was drawn
through the streets, lined with thousands of people.
With it walked the pall-bearers: Craigavon, stoically
impassive, looking elderly as the breeze stirred his
wisps of white hair; Spender, the Englishman who
had devoted his life to Carson's cause; Crawford, who
had brought the guns to Larne; Dawson Bates, the
grey eminence of the Ulster movement. Lady Carson
led the family mourners. The procession stopped for
a few minutes outside the Old Town Hall, which had
been the headquarters of the Ulster Volunteer Force,
and again at the City Hall, where he had signed the
Ulster Covenant. In the cathedral the service was led
by his friend Primate D'Arcy. The coffin was lowered
into the tomb, and from a silver bowl soil from each
of the six counties was scattered on it. Buglars sounded
the Last Post and Reveille, and then the congregation
took up the hymn which had become the Ulster
anthem: 'O God, Our Help in Ages Past'.[9]

5

So 'Sir Edward' came home to his people. For the
biographer it is the meet conclusion to his narrative.
The historian, however, might ask the question: was
it home, or, in a sense, exile? Carson was a more com-

plex figure than either his enemies or his friends were prepared to allow. Within him powerful conflicting tendencies were held in equipoise, and the resulting tension was the driving force of his life. He was, no doubt, ambitious, but he seems genuinely to have lacked political ambition, and it is still something of a mystery that such a man should have attained high office, and wielded so much influence at critical moments, most strikingly at the time of Asquith's downfall in 1916. 'The moment Asquith's fall was accomplished', wrote Beaverbrook of him, 'a kind of incuriousness seemed to descend on him. He was like a man whose task is accomplished. He made no claim for himself.'[10] It is difficult, too, to explain adequately the antithesis summed up succinctly in A. J. P. Taylor's verdict: 'Dangerous in opposition, he was ineffective in office.'[11] Some light is thrown on this enigma if we recall what Carson once told Lloyd George: 'I have remained a lawyer first and a politician afterwards.'[12] Had he never gone into politics, he would, after all, still be remembered as one of the last of the great advocates in the old flamboyant style, and he carried the forensic skill and make-believe into the political arena. He disliked politics, and in the end was disgusted by them. In a sense he never understood them, for they involved the negation of those very qualities on which he placed most value: loyalty, honesty, consistency and truthfulness. Politics could never be for him, as for Lloyd George, simply the art of the possible.

He always asserted that it was only for Ireland that he was in politics, and in this fact lies the key to most of the apparent contradictions in his attitudes. At his funeral service the choir had sung his own favourite hymn: 'I Vow to Thee, My Country'. His was indeed the love that never faltered, the love prepared to pay the price — but which was his country? 'He has no

country, only a caste' was the taunt of one of his
critics, and it may seem truer today than when it was
uttered. At the time it was indignantly rejected, however, for the Union was not yet a lost cause, and
Carson had no intention of losing it. T. M. Healy took
a juster view when he said of him: 'Although a Unionist, he was never un-Irish.'[13] It was true, and it was
clearly shown in his attitudes to issues which were not
directly concerned with the Union, in his support, for
example, for the establishment of a Catholic university
in Ireland, or for the return of Sir Hugh Lane's pic-
tures to Dublin. If a patriot is a man who loves his
country, then Carson was a patriot, though he would
have disclaimed the narrower political connotation.
He sincerely believed that his country could only be
prosperous and happy as part of the United Kingdom,
to which he gave his supreme allegiance. The Union
was his lodestar, and when it set he plumbed depths
of bitterness and defeat which even his followers
could not measure. It was no part of his intention to
dismember Ireland, or to see Unionism survive in the
form of a Home Rule parliament in Belfast — rather
the contrary was true — but having used the resistance
of the Ulster loyalists as the trump card to defeat
Home Rule, he became to some degree their prisoner.
Paradoxically, the very success of the Ulster cause
ensured the ruin of his own. He was in his day, and
will long remain, a figure of controversy, since, as Dr
Johnson observed, the Irish 'never speak well of one
another'; but his courage, honesty and integrity were
beyond cavil, and it could not be said of him that he
ever chose the easy way. His epitaph might be in the
words he once wrote to Lady Londonderry: 'I have
always walked up hill with the collar hurting.'

References

CP = Carson Papers
UUCP = Ulster Unionist Council Papers

Introduction (pp. 1—2)
  1. *Annual Register*, 1935.

Chapter 1: An Irish Barrister (pp. 3—18)
  1. For Carson's childhood and family background see Marjoribanks, *Carson*, I, 1—16; Hyde, *Carson*, 4—13; Savory, 'Carson', *DNB* (20th century, 1931—40), 146.
  2. Hyde, 495.
  3. *Ibid.*, 14; Farson, *The Man Who Wrote 'Dracula'*, 18, 23.
  4. Hyde, 15.
  5. *Ibid.*, 26.
  6. Marjoribanks, I, 62—3.

Chapter 2: 'Coercion Carson' (pp. 19—30)
  1. Cooke and Vincent, *The Governing Passion*, 448.
  2. Marjoribanks, I, 105—6.
  3. Dugdale, *Balfour*, I, 141—3; Young, *Balfour*, 106—8.
  4. Dugdale, I, 147; Hyde, 76.
  5. Blunt, *The Land War in Ireland*, 365.
  6. Hyde, 77—8.
  7. Marjoribanks, I, 95.

Chapter 3: The Guiding Star (pp. 31—56)
  1. Lyons, *Dillon*, 92, 250.
  2. Marjoribanks, I, 137.
  3. Hyde, 109.
  4. *Ibid.*, 116.
  5. Marjoribanks, I, 163—4.
  6. *Ibid.*, 189—90.
  7. *Ibid.*, 191—231; Hyde, 126—44.
  8. Dugdale, I, 245.
  9. Hyde, 152.

Chapter 4: Sir Edward (pp. 57–76)

[136]

1. CP, D1507/1900.
2. Marjoribanks, I, 288–97.
3. *Ibid.*, 298–305.
4. Hyde, 186–7.
5. Biggs-Davison, *Wyndham*, 176.
6. Reading, *Isaacs*, I, 161–2.
7. Marjoribanks, I, 416–45.
8. 8 Dec. 1907, Hyde, 239; Wilson, *Campbell-Bannerman*, 116.
9. Hyde, 258.
10. *Ibid.*, 286.
11. Ervine, *Craigavon*, 185.
12. Ryan, *Mutiny at the Curragh*, 18; Hyde, 291.
13. Hyde, 293–6; Chamberlain, *Politics from the Inside*, 373, 375–6, 388; Petrie, *Chamberlain*, I, 300–7.
14. Hyde, 297.

Chapter 5: 'King Carson' (pp. 77–92)

1. Shaw, *The Matter with Ireland*, 79; for a detailed account of the 'Ulster crisis' see Stewart, *The Ulster Crisis*, and Ryan.
2. Buckland, *Documents*, 224 (copy signed by Carson).
3. *Ibid.*, 14.
4. Spender Papers, D1295.
5. UUCP, D1327; Stewart, 76–8.
6. Hyde, 329.
7. Donaldson, *The Marconi Scandal*, 94–6; Reading, I, 326–75; Churchill, *The World Crisis: The Aftermath*, 552–5.
8. UUCP, D1327/1–9, *passim.*
9. *Ibid.*, D1327/4/8; O'Neill Papers, D1238/1.
10. UUCP, D1327/4/21; Crawford Papers, D640/27–30.
11. Crawford Papers, D1700.
12. Colvin, *Carson*, II, 241–2.
13. Gollin, *Proconsul in Politics*, 186; Wrench, *Milner*, 287.
14. Colvin, II, 193.
15. Hyde, 339.
16. Crozier, *Impressions and Recollections*, 143–4.
17. Lady Spender's Diary, 20 Mar. 1914, D1633.
18. Hyde, 355.
19. Crawford's Diary, 26–30 Mar. 1914, Crawford Papers, D1700.
20. Memo by Sir Frank Hall (Buckland, *Documents*, 253).

Chapter 6: Facing the Music (pp. 93–121)

1. O'Neill Papers, D1238 (letter of Frank Hall, 10 Aug. 1914, [137] concerning enlistment of the Volunteers: 'Carson must be satisfied with the situation in regard to Ulster'); Hyde, 379–80.
2. Hyde, 380–2.
3. Colvin, III, 37. Lady Carson's uncle Moreton Frewen, who was a Home Ruler, was astonished and dismayed at the marriage. (Leslie, *Mr Frewen of England*, 171, 176, 185)
4. CP, D1507/1914.
5. Trevelyan, *Grey of Fallodon*, 302 (conversation between Grey and Gilbert Murray).
6. Beaverbrook, *Politicians*, II, 162; CP, D1507/1915.
7. Hyde, 395.
8. CP, D1507/1916; Hyde, 399–400.
9. Lady Spender's Diary, 23 Mar. 1916, D1633.
10. Beaverbrook, *Men and Power*, 144–5.
11. Hyde, 401.
12. Beaverbrook, *Politicians*, II, 289, 293–8.
13. Hyde, 411.
14. *Ibid.*, 413.
15. Lloyd George, *War Memoirs*, III, 1175–6.
16. Beaverbrook, *Men and Power*, 145–6.
17. CP, D1507/1917. Marder states that the King suggested to Lloyd George that Carson should go to the Admiralty instead of Milner. (*From Dreadnought to Scapa Flow*, III, 341n)
18. For Haig's intrigues against Carson see Marder, IV, 200; Beaverbrook, *Men and Power*, 163–6.
19. CP, D1507/4/154–7/1917.
20. *Ibid.*, D1507/4/152, 154, 167/1917; Riddell, *War Diary*, 243.
21. Marder, IV, 199–200.
22. CP, D1507/1917.
23. Lloyd George, III, 1177.
24. CP, D1507/1917.
25. *Ibid.*; see also Marder, IV, 157, 161.
26. CP, D1507/5/32/1917.
27. Smith, *Buchan*, 209, 213; Colvin, II, 278.
28. Buckland, *Irish Unionism* 1, 120–1.
29. Hyde, 428–9; *Irish Times*, 4 Dec. 1918.
30. Hyde, 431–2.
31. UUCP, D1327/3/21.
32. CP, D1507/1918.

[138] 33. Crawford Papers, D1700.
       34. Hyde, 449.
       35. CP, D1507/1921.

Chapter 7: Betrayal (pp. 122—134)
   1. Hyde, 446.
   2. *Ibid.*, 463—6.
   3. Birkenhead, *Birkenhead*, II, 163—5.
   4. Beckett in Martin, ed., *Leaders and Men*, 90.
   5. Jones, *Whitehall Diary*, III, 189.
   6. Hyde, 474.
   7. *Ibid.*, 486—9.
   8. Ervine, 497, 526, 538.
   9. *Belfast Telegraph*, 26 Oct. 1935.
  10. Beaverbrook, *Politicians*, II, 355.
  11. Taylor, *English History, 1914—1945*, 31n.
  12. Hyde, 1.
  13. Marjoribanks, I, 9.

Select Bibliography

The authorised biography of Carson was begun in his lifetime by Edward Marjoribanks and was originally intended to be in two volumes. Marjoribanks had completed the first volume by 1932 when he tragically took his own life, and the work was completed in two further volumes by Ian Colvin. This three-volume biography (London 1932–36) is the fullest and most detailed, but H. Montgomery Hyde's *Carson* (London 1953; repr. London 1979) is more accurate and has the advantage of drawing on papers which had become available since 1936 and on the correspondence of Lady Londonderry. There are also some short biographical sketches of Carson by his contemporaries which may be conveniently listed here:

Bates, J. V., *Sir Edward Carson*, with an Introduction by the Rt Hon. A. J. Balfour and a Foreword by James Craig, London 1921

Birkenhead, F. E. Smith, 1st Earl of, *Contemporary Personalities*, London 1924

Comyn-Platt, Sir Thomas, 'The Ulster Leader' in *National Review*, Oct. 1913

Moles, T. H., *Lord Carson of Duncairn*, with a Foreword by Sir James Craig, Belfast 1925

Savory, Sir Douglas L., 'Lord Carson' in *Dictionary of National Biography*

The verdict of two distinguished Irish historians on Carson's significance in Irish history may be found in:

Beckett, J. C., 'Carson – Unionist and Rebel' in F. X. Martin, ed., *Leaders and Men of the Easter Rising: Dublin 1916*, London 1967 (repr. in J. C. Beckett, *Confrontations: Studies in Irish History*, London 1972)

McDowell, R. B., 'Edward Carson' in Conor Cruise O'Brien, ed., *The Shaping of Modern Ireland*, London 1960

Invaluable for the background of Irish Unionism in the period are the two volumes of Dr Patrick Buckland's scholarly study:

Irish Unionism 1: *The Anglo-Irish and the New Ireland, 1885–1922*, Dublin 1972

Irish Unionism 2: *Ulster Unionism and the Origins of Northern Ireland, 1886–1922*, Dublin 1973

and his volume of documents, *Irish Unionism, 1885–1923: A Documentary History*, Belfast 1973

Carson the man, and the commanding position he occupied in legal and political life, are discussed in the memoirs of many of his contemporaries and in scores of other works of history. To attempt to list even a large proportion of them would require as much space as the text, but the titles of those cited in reference notes are included in the select bibliography below. In writing this new brief biography I have also used material from the Carson Papers, now in the Public Record Office of Northern Ireland, and from other collections of papers deposited there. These are:

Ulster Unionist Council Papers (D1327)
Crawford Papers (D640 and D1700)
Spender Papers (D1295 and D1633)
O'Neill Papers (D1238)
Hall Papers (D1540)
Craigavon Papers (Lady Craigavon's Diary) (D1415)

The Carson Papers are incomplete and are in the process of being recalendered. They comprise about 3,000 documents which survived the destruction of his papers in an air raid on London—miscellaneous correspondence, some Irish and cabinet papers and other items. They are useful for some episodes of his career, but most of the interesting correspondence is missing and there are no legal records.

Addison, Christopher, *Four and a Half Years*, 2 vols, London 1934

Beaverbrook, Max Aitken, Lord, *Politicians and the War, 1914–1916*, 2 vols, London 1928

Beaverbrook, Max Aitken, Lord, *Men and Power, 1917–1918*, London 1956

Biggs-Davison, John N., *George Wyndham*, London 1951

Birkenhead, Frederick, 2nd Earl of, *Frederick Edwin, Earl of Birkenhead*, 2 vols, London 1959

Blake, Robert, *The Unknown Prime Minister*, London 1955

Blunt, Wilfrid S., *The Land War in Ireland*, London 1912

Chamberlain, Sir Austen, *Politics from the Inside*, London 1936

Churchill, W. S., *The World Crisis: The Aftermath*, London 1929

Cooke, A. B., and Vincent, J. R., *The Governing Passion: Cabinet Government and Party Politics in Britain, 1885–86*, Brighton 1974

Crawford, Frederick H., *Guns for Ulster*, Belfast 1947

Crozier, F. P., *Impressions and Recollections*, London 1930

Donaldson, Frances, *The Marconi Scandal*, London 1962

Dugdale, Blanche E. C., *Arthur James Balfour, First Earl Balfour*, 2 vols, London 1936

Ervine, St John, *Craigavon, Ulsterman*, London 1949

Esher, Reginald Brett, Viscount, *Journals and Letters*, Vol. IV (1916–30), London 1938

Farson, Daniel, *The Man Who Wrote 'Dracula'*, London 1975

Fergusson, Sir James, *The Curragh Incident*, London 1964

Gollin, A. M., *Proconsul in Politics: A Study of Lord Milner in Opposition and Power*, London 1964

Gwynn, Denis, *The Life of John Redmond*, London 1932

Hastings, Sir Patrick, *Autobiography*, London 1948

Jellicoe, John, Earl, *The Crisis of the Naval War*, London 1920

Jones, Thomas, *Whitehall Diary*, Vol. III: *Ireland, 1918–1925*, ed. Keith Middlemas, London 1971

Leslie, Anita, *Mr Frewen of England: a Victorian Adventurer*, London 1966

Lloyd George, David, *War Memoirs*, 6 vols, London 1933–36

Lyons, F. S. L., *John Dillon*, London 1968

Marder, A. J., *From Dreadnought to Scapa Flow: The Royal Navy in the Fisher Era, 1904–1919*, Vols III–IV, London 1966–69

McNeill, Ronald, *Ulster's Stand for Union*, London 1922

O'Brien, Peter, Lord, *Reminiscences*, London 1916

Petrie, Sir Charles, *Life and Letters of the Rt Hon. Sir Austen Chamberlain*, 2 vols, London 1939–40

Reading, Gerald Isaacs, 2nd Marquess of, *Rufus Isaacs, First Marquess of Reading*, 2 vols, London 1942–45

Riddell, George, Lord, *War Diary, 1914–1918*, London 1933

Roskill, Stephen, *Hankey, Man of Secrets*, Vol. I (1877–1918), London 1970

Ross, Sir John, *The Years of my Pilgrimage*, London 1924

Ryan, A. P., *Mutiny at the Curragh*, London 1956

Shaw, G. B., *The Matter with Ireland*, London 1962

Simon, John, Viscount, *Retrospect*, London 1952

Smith, Janet Adam, *John Buchan*, London 1965

Stewart, A. T. Q., *The Ulster Crisis*, London 1967 (repr. London 1979)

Taylor, A. J. P., *English History, 1914–1945*, Oxford 1965

[142] Trevelyan, G. M., *Grey of Fallodon*, London 1937

Wilson, John, *CB: A Life of Sir Henry Campbell-Bannerman*, London 1973

Wrench, Sir Evelyn, *Alfred, Lord Milner*, London 1958

Young, Kenneth, *Arthur James Balfour*, London 1963

Annual Register
Belfast Telegraph
Dictionary of National Biography
Irish Times
The Times

Index

Abberline, Chief Inspector, 60
Abercorn, Duchess of, 97
Abyssinia, 1
Adair, Gen. Sir William, 88
Admiralty, 65, 66, 67, 87, 97, 107–8, 109, 110, 111, 112, 113
Aitken, Sir Max (Lord Beaverbrook), 105, 108, 133
Alaska, 61
Albemarle, HMS, 68
Ambrose Light, 1
Amending Bill (1914), 95, 103, 118
America, *see* United States of America
American Air Lines, 1
Anna Karenina, 2
Anglo-Irish War, 118
Anthony, Miss, 14, 15, 16
antimony poisoning, 59–60
Antrim, Co., 86, 88, 91, 122
Archer-Shee case, 64–7
Archer-Shee, George 64–8
Archer-Shee, Martin, 67
Ards peninsula, 91
Arlington House, 4, 5, 6
Armagh, Co., 3, 81
armistice, 116
Articles of Agreement for a Treaty between Great Britain and Ireland, 123, 125, 127, 128, 129
Ashbourne, Lord, 9
Asquith, Herbert Henry (Lord Oxford), 33, 38, 40, 69, 72, 77, 79, 83, 86, 87, 91, 92, 93, 94, 95, 96, 97, 100, 102, 103, 104, 105, 106, 118, 133
astrology, 120, 131
Athenry, 3
Atkinson, John, 28, 32, 62
Atlantic Ocean, 1, 95

Australia, 1
Austria, 98, 99
Auxiliary Division, 122

'bagwomen', 8
Balcarres, Lord, 75
Baldwin, Stanley, 55
Balfour, Arthur James (Lord), 21, 22, 25, 26, 27, 28, 31, 32, 34, 35, 36, 38, 40, 43, 46, 52, 53, 57, 58, 71, 72, 74, 75, 101, 105, 106, 107, 108, 111, 124, 129; C.'s opinion of, 26–7; opinion of C., 27; Prime Minister, 62–3
Balfour, Gerald, 52
Balkans, 98–100
Ballad of Reading Gaol, The, 52
Ballykinlar, 96
Balmoral, 86
Baltic, 90
Bangor, Co. Down, 91
Barbavilla House, 16
Bar library, 8
Barton, Robert, 123
Bates, Sir Dawson, 132
Beaverbrook, Lord, *see* Aitken, Sir Max
Bedford, Duke of, 85
Belfast, 1, 2, 74, 77, 82, 87, 88, 89, 90, 91, 115, 116, 122, 128, 131, 132, 134
Belfast Lough, 73, 87, 132
Belgium, 115
Big Ben, 37
Birchington, 101, 110
Birkenhead, Lord, *see* Smith, F. E.
Birrell, Augustine, 97, 127
Black and Tans, 122
Bluebird, 1
Blunt, Wilfrid Scawen, 28
Board of Trade, 69

[144]

Boer War, *see* South African War
Bonar Law, Andrew, 75, 76, 77, 86, 95, 97, 99, 100, 102, 104, 105, 106, 107, 130
Boundary Commission, 127
boxing, 46
Boyd, Dr Walter, 17
Bramley, Mr, 9
Brennan, John, 16
British army, 79, 82, 83, 85
British Empire, 78, 81
Broke, HMS, 132
Brook, H. L., 1
Bruce-Porter, Sir Bruce, 75
Buchan, John (Lord Tweedsmuir), 113
Buckingham Palace, 92, 107
Bulgaria, 98
Burke, Edmund, 4, 6
Burke, Thomas, 16
Burne-Jones, Sir Edward, 55
Burne-Jones, Philip, 55
Bury St, 39, 53
Butt, Isaac, 6, 9

Cadogan Hotel, 51
Cambridge, 21
Campbell, J. H. (Lord Glenavy), 7, 75
Campbell, Sir Malcolm, 1
Campbell-Bannerman, Sir Henry, 63
Canada, 62, 75, 76
Cap Gris Nez, 1
'Captain Moonlight', 16
Capuchin Order, 33
Carlton Club, 34, 39
Carrickfergus, 87
Carson, Aileen, 13, 31, 67, 74, 90, 131
Carson, Annette (first Lady Carson), 11, 12, 13, 18, 20, 29, 30, 39, 55, 60, 61, 66, 67, 79, 80
Carson, Bella (sister), 13
Carson, Edward (son), 121, 130, 131
Carson, Edward Henry (father), 3, 4, 5, 9, 12
Carson, Gladys Isobel (daughter), 18, 31, 68, 130
Carson, Isabella (mother, 3–4, 10, 14–15
Carson, Ruby (second Lady Carson), 95, 107, 112, 121, 127, 131, 132

Carson, Walter Seymour (son), 31, 61, 68, 131
Carson, William Henry Lambert (son 'Harry'), 12, 31, 55, 68, 122, 130
Castle Comer, 11
Castle Ellen, 3, 10
Catholic university, 56, 134
Cavendish, Lord Frederick, 16
Cecil, Lady Blanche, 21
chalbeate springs, 60
Chamberlain, Austen, 38, 72, 75, 123, 125–6, 129, 130
Chamberlain, Joseph, 19, 38, 52, 129
Chancery, Court of, 8, 39
Chapman, George (Severin Klosowski), 59–60
Charlton Musgrave, 95
Cherry, Richard, 7
Chesterton, Cecil, 81
Chesterton, G. K., 81
Christian Brothers, 15
Church of Ireland, 3, 4, 6
Churchill, Lord Randolph, 69, 71
Churchill, Sir Winston, 69, 81, 86, 87, 97, 130
Churchill, Lady, 130
City Hall, Belfast, 132
Clandeboye, 96
Clanrickarde, Lord, 33, 37
Clare, Co., 59
Clark, Sir George, 83
Clarke, Sir Edward, 39, 48, 50, 51, 54
Cleethorpes, 1
Cleve Court, 122, 130
Clouds of Witness, 58
Clyde, Firth of, 87
Clydevalley, s.s., 91
coercion policy, 16, 19–30
Coercion Act (1881), 16
Coleraine, 76
College Green, 5
Collins, Michael, 123
Committee of Imperial Defence, 93
Common Pleas, Court of, 8
Commons, House of, 35–8, 40–2, 45, 52, 70, 88, 101, 102, 109, 121
Communism, 2
conscription, 102, 115, 116
Conservative Party, 19, 32, 42, 45, 46, 52, 53, 62, 71, 72, 74, 75, 76, 77, 85, 88, 93, 95, 97, 100,

104, 105, 106, 123, 125, 127;
C. as possible leader of, 74—6
Convention, Irish (1917—18), 113—
15, 116
convoy system, 109, 110
Cork, 15, 26
Cork, Co., 22
Cosgrave, William, 129
Council of Ireland, 118
county option, 87
Covenant, see Ulster Covenant
Craig, James (Lord Craigavon),
72, 73, 83, 87, 88, 89, 90,
91, 94, 115, 117, 125, 131,
132
Craig, Mrs (Lady Craigavon), 89
Craigavon House, 73, 78, 79, 82,
89, 90, 91
Crawford, Maj. F. H., 82, 83, 84,
90, 91
Criminal Law Amendment Act
(1887), 22—7, 33, 35, 68
Cripps, Alfred, 57
Croce, B., 113
Cromwell, Oliver, 3, 6
cross-examination (C.'s methods),
7, 9—10, 39, 41, 48—50, 51,
63, 64, 66
Crozier, Gen. F. P., 88
'Curragh Incident', 89
Curzon, Lord, 105, 107, 124, 126,
128

Dáil Éireann, 117, 118, 123
Daily Express, 38
Daily News, 109
Daily Telegraph, 109
Dalkey, 31
Danube, River, 99
D'Arcy, Abp Charles, 132
Dardanelles, 2, 97—100
Darling, Sir Charles, 34—5, 43, 54
Davey, Maj. W. H., 117
Daytona Beach, 1
de Gaulle, Gen. Charles, 24
Denmark, 90
'Denver, Duke of', 58
detective novels, 2, 131
de Valera, Eamon, 2, 133
Devlin, Joseph, 89
'devolution crisis', 62
Devon, 120
Dillon, John, 25, 33, 40, 117
disestablishment, 6
Doctor Johnson's Buildings, 35,
39, 54, 118

Donaghadee, 91
Donegal, Co., 33, 92
Dorset St, 16
Douglas, Lord Alfred, 46, 49
Down, Co., 72, 86
Downing St, 104, 110
Dracula, 6
Dreyfus case, 64
Dublin, 2, 3—14, 16, 18, 20, 28,
29, 31, 36, 39, 40, 48, 54, 62,
70, 102, 117, 134
Dublin Castle, 22, 24, 26, 28, 33
Dublin University, see Trinity Col-
lege
Duffy, Charles Gavan, 123
Dugdale, Blanche, 27, 129—30
Duggan, Eamon, 123
Dumfries, 3
Duncairn, 116, 122
Dundee, 69, 73
Durham, Co., 45

Earhart, Amelia, 1
Easter Rising, 102—3, 113
Eaton Place, 128
Edward VII, 57, 58, 60
Egypt, 100
elections, 19, 31, 32, 40, 52, 58,
63, 68—9, 70, 71, 72, 116—17
Elgar, Sir Edward, 85
Eliot, T. S., 2
Emmet, Robert, 6
English Channel, 1, 96
Enniskillen, 78, 87
Eton College, 130
Euston, 88
Evening News, 39, 44
Evicted Tenants Commission,
33—4, 35, 37, 44
Exchequer, Court of, 8

Fanny, s.s., 90—1
federalism, 71
Fermanagh, Co., 78, 92, 94
Fermoy, 23
Finner, 96
First World War, 2, 67, 68, 92,
93—116
Fisher, Admiral Lord, 97
Flanders, 98
Florida, 1
Forster, W. E., 21
Four Courts, 6—7, 32, 34, 40
France, 52, 93, 96, 110
French Revolution, 6
Freud, Sigmund, 2
Frewen, Ruby, see Carson, Ruby

Gallipoli, 98, 99, 100
Galway, 58

[146] Galway, Co., 3
Garbo, Greta, 2
Garvin, J. L., 109
Gaudy Night, 2
Geddes, Sir Eric, 110, 111
general elections, *see* elections
George III, 39
George V, 2, 80, 86, 92, 94, 106,
    122, 123
George, David Lloyd, *see* Lloyd
    George, David
Germany, 85, 90, 92, 98, 99, 115
Gibson, Edward, *see* Ashbourne,
    Lord
Gill, Charles, 101
Gillon, Stair, 113
Gladstone, William Ewart, 13, 19,
    32–3, 39, 40, 41, 42, 70
Glasgow, 76
Glenavy, Lord, *see* Campbell, J. H.
'God Save Ireland', 29
Goulding, Sir Edward, 93
Gough, Gen. Sir Hubert, 89, 112
Government of Ireland Act (1920),
    see Home Rule Bill (4th)
Grafton St, 5
Grainger, –, 50
Grattan, Henry, 6
Great War, *see* First World War
Green St, 8, 31
Griffith, Arthur, 123
gun-running, 82, 83, 84, 90–1
Gweedore, 33, 35
Gwynne, H. A., 109

Haig, Field-Marshal Sir Douglas
    (Lord), 108, 112
Hall, Col. Frank, 91
Halsbury, Lord, 47
Halsey, Admiral Sir Lionel, 111
Hamburg, 83, 84, 90
Hamilton, Gen. Sir Ian, 98, 99
Hampshire, HMS, 103
Harcourt, Sir William, 41, 42, 127
Harcourt St, 3, 4
Harmsworth, Sir Alfred, *see* North-
    cliffe, Lord
Hawkins, Sir Henry, 44
Healy, T. M., 29, 68, 82, 134
Henderson, Arthur, 107
Herbert Place, 11, 12
Herepath, Mr (C.'s clerk), 54
Herschell, Lord, 44
Hicks Beach, Sir Michael, 21

Historical Society, Trinity College,
    6, 7
Hitler, Adolf, 1
Hobbes, Thomas, 78
Holyhead, 11
Holywood, Co. Down, 87
Homburg, 60, 81, 85, 96
Home Rule, 9, 19, 20, 33, 40, 52,
    62, 68, 70, 71, 72, 75, 77, 82,
    85–6, 87, 114, 116, 134
Home Rule Bills: (1st, 1886), 19;
    (2nd, 1893), 33, 40, 42, 70;
    (3rd, 1912), 70, 77, 79, 80,
    84, 94, 95, 103, 114, 118;
    (4th, 1920), 118, 119, 120,
    126
hurling, 6

Importance of Being Earnest, The
    47
indemity fund, 79
Indian army, 78
Inns of Court, 7
Irish Brigade, 58
Irish Convention (1917–18), *see*
    Convention
Irish Free State, 7, 126, 128, 129
Irish Mail 90,
Irish National League, 22
Irish Parliamentary Party, 19, 20,
    23, 32, 36, 41, 68, 70, 71, 105,
    117
Irish Privy Council, 52
Irish Republican Army, 122, 123,
    124
Irish Sea, 7–8, 34
Irish Volunteers, 92
Isaacs, Sir Rufus (Lord Reading),
    54, 63–4, 66, 67, 81, 117

'Jack the Ripper', 60
James I, 86
Jameson, Dr Leander Starr, 54
'Jameson Raid', 55
'Jehu Junior', 43
Jersey City, 60
Jellicoe, Admiral Sir John, 108,
    109, 110, 111, 112
Johnson, Dr Samuel, 134; *see*
    Doctor Johnson's Buildings
Jubilee, 2

Kaiser, the, *see* William II
Kenny, William, 34
Kent, 1, 122
Kiel Canal, 90

Kildare, Co., 89
Kildare Street Club, 16, 54
Kilkenny, Co., 11
Kilmainham Jail, 16
Kingstown, 11
Kingston, Countess of, 22
Kipling, Rudyard, 55, 80, 85
Kirwan, Annette, *see* Carson, Annette
Kitchener, Field-Marshal Lord, 93–4, 98, 99, 103
Klosowski, Severin, *see* Chapman, George

Labouchere, Henry, 23, 25
Labour Party, 105, 107, 129
Lambert, Isabella, *see* Carson, Isabella
Lambert, John, 3
Lambert, Katherine, 10
Lambert, Capt. Peter, 3
Lamlash, 87
Land Act (1881), 13
Land League, 14, 16, 18
landlords, 13, 22, 33–4, 37–8, 52
Larne, 91
Law, Andrew Bonar, *see* Bonar Law, Andrew
Lawson, J. A., 16
League of Nations, 2
Lecky, W. E. H., 6
Leinster Circuit, 8, 13, 75
Lewis, Mr, 38
Liberal Party, 19, 20, 23, 25, 32–3, 39, 41, 44, 63, 68, 69, 70, 71, 81, 100
Liberal Unionists, 19, 20, 32
Liverpool, 72
Lloyd George, David, 69, 71, 72, 81, 99, 100, 103, 104, 105, 106; Prime Minister, 107–18, 121, 122, 123, 127, 130, 133; and Government of Ireland Act (1920), 118–19; and the Treaty, 123, 127; C.'s opinion of, 112, 130
Logan, J. W., 41
Long, Walter, 70, 74, 75, 97
London, 1, 7, 11, 39, 46, 54, 55, 67, 82, 84, 89, 91, 117
London and North-Eastern Railway, 110
Londonderry, 82, 88
Londonderry House, 44, 45, 128
Londonderry, Lady, 20–1, 44, 45, 68, 69, 71, 74, 75, 80, 97, 115, 117, 134
Londonderry, Lord, 20, 44, 118
Lonsdale, J. B., 70
Lords, House of, 42, 45, 58, 69, 70, 71, 121, 122, 123–6
Loreburn, Lord, 85
Los Angeles, 1
Lunacy Commissioner, 15
Lynch, Col. Arthur, 58, 59

Macclesfield, 69
MacDonald, Ramsay, 129
MacDonnell, Sir Antony, 62
McKenna, Reginald, 105
MacMahon, Joseph, 16
MacNabb, Dr H. N., 117
Macready, Gen. Sir Nevil, 87
Mahaffy, J. P., 5, 116
Mahon, Gen. Sir Bryan, 98
Mandeville, John, 22
Mansion House, Dublin, 29, 117
'Marconi scandal', 81
Margate, 122
Market Harborough, 41
Marlborough, Duke of, 6
Martin, Thomas, 16
Mathew, Sir James, 33
Mathew, Fr Theobald, 33
Matin, Le, 81
Menin Gate, 67
Merrifield, L. S., 131
Merrion Square, 18, 29, 30
Metropole Hotel, Monte Carlo, 60
Mexico City, 1
Middle Temple, 7, 34, 35, 39, 57
Midleton, Lord, 114
Milner, Lord, 85, 106, 107
Minster, Kent, 122
Mitchelstown, 22, 23–6
Monkstown, 11
Monte Carlo, 60
Morley, John, 33, 35, 36, 37, 41. 44, 124
Morning Post, 101
Moss Brothers, 94
Mount Stewart, 45
Mourne Mts, 73, 128
Murder in the Cathedral, 2
Mussolini, Benito, 1

Nation, The, 29
National League, 22, 29
National Liberal Club, 20
National University of Ireland, 56
navy, 64–7, 68, 87; *see also* Admiralty

New Brunswick, 76
Newcastle-upon-Tyne, 1
[148] Newry, 87, 102
Newtownards, 96
New York, 1
Nigeria, 104
Normandie, 1
Northcliffe, Lord, 109
Northern Ireland, 86, 113, 118–19, 120, 122, 128, 131, 132; *see also* partition, Ulster
North Sea, 90

O'Brien, Peter (Lord O'Brien of Kilfenora), 18, 30, 43, 54
O'Brien, William, 22, 23, 24, 26, 34, 54
Observer, The, 109
O'Connor, Charles, 7
'O God, Our Help in Ages Past', 77, 132
Old Bailey, 50
Old Testament, 1
Old Town Hall, Belfast, 79, 88, 132
Oliver, F. S., 71
Omagh, 87
Orangeism, 1, 72, 73, 81, 82, 116, 118
Orkney Is, 103
Osborne, Royal Naval College, 64, 68
'Ossa' (C.'s nickname), 5
Oxford, 5, 50, 61

'packing' of juries, 18
Page, Walter Hines, 113
Paget, Gen. Sir Arthur, 89
Pall Mall Gazette, 38
Paris, 52
Parker, Charles, 47, 49, 50
Park Lane, 44
parliament, 19–20, 21–2, 23, 31–2, 35–8, 40, 41–2, 45, 52–3, 55–6, 58, 59, 60, 61, 62, 63, 68, 69, 70, 71, 72, 77, 78, 79, 81, 82, 84, 87, 88, 93, 94, 95, 96–7, 101, 102, 104, 105, 106–7, 109, 116–17, 119, 120, 121, 122, 123–7, 128, 129, 130, 133; of Northern Ireland, 119–20, 122, 131; *see also* Commons, Lords
Parliament Act (1911), 70
Parnell, Charles Stewart, 16, 19, 21, 32

partition, 86–7, 113, 117, 126, 127, 134
Peel, Sir Robert, 72
'People's Budget' (1909), 69
'Peter the Packer', *see* O'Brien, Peter
Phoenix Park murders, 16, 17
Pitt, William (the Younger), 4
'Plan of Campaign', 22, 23, 27, 33
Plantation of Ulster, 86
Plunkett, David, 32
poisoning, murder by, 59
Poland, 60
Portarlington, 4, 5, 98
Portora Royal School, 5
Powell, Maj.-Gen. C. H., 96
Presbyterians, 76, 77, 119
Probate, Divorce and Admiralty Division (of the High Court), 62
Punch, 29, 41

Queen's Bench, Court of, 8
Queensbury, Marquess of, 46, 47, 51
Q-ships, 109

Radicals, 14, 19, 101
Rattigan, Sir Terence, 64
'Rawbones' (C.'s nickname), 5
Reading, Lord, *see* Isaacs, Sir Rufus
Redmond, John, 41, 70, 86, 87, 92, 93, 94, 97, 113, 114, 115, 117
Republic of Ireland, 129; *see also* Irish Free State
Rex v. Krause, 58
Rhineland, 60
Rhodes, Cecil, 68
Rhodesia, 68
Rice, Rev. James, 4
Richardson, Gen. Sir George, 78, 96
Robertson, Field-Marshal Sir William, 99
Roche, John, 33, 37–8
Ross, John, 7, 10
Rottingdean, 55, 80
Royal Irish Constabulary, 11, 25, 26, 122
Royal Naval College, 64
Royal Navy, *see* navy
Russell, Sir Charles, 39, 45
Russell, Charles, 45, 46, 47
Russell, Earl, 58

Russia, 93
Rutland Gate, 55

St Anne's Cathedral, Belfast, 132
St James's St, 39
St Stephen's Green, 4, 5
Salisbury, Lord, 19, 20, 27, 32, 40, 52, 57, 62
Salonika, 99
Samuel, Herbert, 81
Sandycove, 5, 11
Saunderson, Col. Edward, 41, 53, 72
Savoy Hotel, 47
Sayers, Dorothy L., 2, 58
Saxons, 43
Scotland, 3, 46, 76, 77, 86, 87
Scotland Yard, 60
Scottish Covenant (1557), 77
Seaford, Sussex, 96
Seely, Col. John (Lord Mottistone), 87
Senate (of the Irish Free State), 7
Serbia, 98, 99, 100
Shannon, James, 6–7, 10–11, 12
Shaw, George Bernard, 24, 77
Shrewsbury, Earl of, 20
Simon, Sir John, 61
Sinn Féin, 114, 115, 117, 123, 124, 127
Slava, River, 99
Slingsby case, 101
Smith, F. E. (Lord Birkenhead), 71, 72, 81, 117, 122, 125, 126, 128, 130
Smythe, Barlow, 17
Smythe, Mrs Helen, 16
'Snuffy Maggie', 8
Solent, 61
Somerset, 95
Somme, Battle of the, 96
South African War, 58, 68
Southampton, 1
South Staffordshire Regiment, 67
Soviet Union, 2
Spender, Lilian, Lady, 89, 101, 102, 107, 115
Spender, Sir Wilfrid, 79, 93, 132
'Spy' cartoon, 43
Stoker, Bram, 6
Stormont, 131
Strand, 46
submarines, 2, 109–12
Sullivan, T.D., 28, 29
Sussex, 96
Suvla Bay, 98

Switzerland, 68

Tailor's Gazette, 38
Tallow, Co. Waterford, 14, 15
Tanner, Dr, 26, 41
tariff reform, 71
Taylor, A. J. P., 133
Taylor, Alfred, 47
Temple, *see* Middle Temple
Tenby, 90
Thames, river, 93
Thanet, Isle of, 101, 122
Thirty-Nine Steps, The, 113
'Tiger Lily' (Balfour's nickname), 21
Times, The, 34, 38, 81, 85
Tite St, 46
Tone, Theobald Wolfe, 6
trade unions, 39
Transvaal, 55
Treaty, Anglo-Irish, *see* Articles of Agreement
Trinity College, Dublin, 3, 5, 6, 8, 31, 32, 46, 48, 52, 63, 75, 113, 116
Tuskar Rock, 91
'Twelfth of July', 1, 116, 118
Tyrone, Co., 92, 94

U-boats, *see* submarines
Ulster, 1, 2, 7, 20, 55, 72, 73, 74, 75, 76, 77–92, 94, 95, 96, 100, 102, 103, 113, 114, 116, 118, 119, 120, 122, 124, 125, 126, 128, 131, 132, 134
Ulster Covenant (1912), 77–8, 79, 80, 92, 119, 125, 132
Ulster Day, 78
Ulster Division, 93–4, 96
Ulster Hall, Belfast, 128
'Ulster provisional government', 79
Ulster Unionist Convention (1892), 40
Ulster Unionist Council, 62, 78, 79, 83, 94–5, 103, 113, 119, 120
Ulster Unionists, 40, 41, 62, 70–7, 81, 83, 92, 93, 94
Ulster Volunteer Force, 78, 79, 80, 81–92, 93, 94, 95, 102, 116, 118, 125, 132
Union (Parliamentary, of Great Britain and Ireland), 14, 19, 20, 32, 71, 74, 79, 92, 127, 132, 134; *see also* Home Rule

[150]

Unionists (Irish), 52, 53, 55, 64, 70, 71, 72, 123, 124, 126, 127–8, 134; Southern Unionists, 92, 113, 114, 115; *see also* Ulster Unionists
United States of America, 1, 60, 61, 62, 103, 111, 112

Vanity Fair, 43
Viceregal Lodge, 20
Victoria, Queen, 53, 57, 85

Wales, Prince of, *see* Edward VII
Wall, Rev. F. H., 4, 11
Wallace, Edgar, 131
war cabinet, 105, 106–7, 108, 110, 111
Wargrave-on-Thames, 93
War Office, 87, 94, 99
Waterford, Co., 13, 14
Webb, Beatrice, 2

Webb, Sydney, 2
Westmeath, Co., 16, 17
Westminster, 31, 34, 40, 62, 82, 93, 117, 120
Westminster Gazette, 57
Whitechapel, 60
Whitehall, 107
white paper, 2
Wilde, Oscar, 5, 43, 46–52
Wilde, Sir William, 5
William II, Kaiser, 85
Wilson, Field-Marshal Sir Henry, 87, 99, 100, 128
Wilson, J. H., 39
Wilson, Woodrow, 103
Wodehouse, P. G., 131
Woolsack, 107, 122, 125
Wyndham, William, 62
Wynyard Park, 45

Yorkshire, 3, 101
Ypres, Battle of, 67